Screenpla

The Art and Business

Asher Garfinkel

ALLWORTH PRESS

NEW YORK

© 2007 Asher Garfinkle

All rights reserved. Copyright under Berne Copyright Convention, Universal Copyright Convention, and Pan-American Copyright Convention. No part of this book may be reproduced, stored in a retrieval system, or transmitted in any form, or by any means, electronic, mechanical, photocopying, recording, or otherwise, without prior permission of the publisher.

11 10 09 08 07   5 4 3 2 1

Published by Allworth Press
An imprint of Allworth Communications, Inc.
10 East 23rd Street, New York, NY 10010

Cover design by Derek Bacchus
Interior design by Mary Belibasakis
Page composition/typography by Integra Software Services, Pvt., Ltd., Pondicherry, India

Library of Congress Cataloging-in-Publication Data

Garfinkel, Asher.
  Screenplay story analysis: the art and business / Asher Garfinkel.
    p. cm.
  Includes bibliographical references and index.
  ISBN-13: 978-1-58115-478-8 (pbk.)
  ISBN-10: 1-58115-478-X
1. Motion picture authorship.   2. Motion picture plays—History and criticism.
I. Title.

  PN1996.G35 2007
  791.43'7—dc22

                                                    2006037364

Contents

Acknowledgments

To all who have asked me over the years, "How do I do that?" this book is first and foremost for you.

Thank you, Professor Sharon Hollenback of Syracuse University, for my very first exposure to coverage, and to Craig Perry for handing me those first few scripts for practice.

I am grateful to the many employers and clients who, over the past number of years, have enabled me to hone my craft and research this book. Extra-special thanks to Peter Medak for his mentorship and friendship.

Enormous gratitude goes out to the following individuals who were generous enough to share their time and wisdom in the form of direct contribution to this book: Michael Bayer, John Cheng, Jerry Drucker, Michael Gilvary, Mitchell Miller, Brian Morewitz, and Craig Perry. Additional thanks to story analysts Brad Dunn, Jay Miles, and Michael Mooradian for their contributions to the coverage examples found in the Appendixes.

I am grateful to UCLA screenwriting professors Hal Ackerman, Tim Albaugh, and Richard Walter and to my thirty or so classmates—all of whom have contributed invaluable depth to my understanding of screenplay fundamentals. Additional gratitude goes out to UCLA producers program instructors Steve Fayne, Tom Garvin, Jim Gianopolous, Geoffrey Gilmore, and Tom Sherak, whose courses added several layers to my comprehension of this dizzying business.

Thanks to my comrades Jason Lewis, Jordan Fox, and James Morris for their encouragement and feedback in the writing of this book.

I am profoundly indebted to my parents, Ruth and Alan Garfinkel, for both the roots and the wings. They also excel as editors. And thanks, Mom, for forcing me to take that typing class in high school.

You would not be reading this were it not for the overwhelming enthusiasm, wisdom, and professionalism of Tad Crawford, Nicole Potter-Talling, Nana Greller, Katie Ellison, and all those at Allworth Press.

Finally, I am eternally grateful to the love of my life, my wife, Wendy, and to our two little superheroes, Isabella and Blake, for making our home the greatest place on earth.

Foreword

First off, congratulations. By purchasing this book, you've just acquired a valuable tool for building your career in Hollywood. Oh, writing coverage might seem mundane or entry level, but as you are about to find out, learning how to write coverage, understanding how it is used by the studio system, and applying these skills to your career path will give you an enormous advantage in this brutally competitive industry.

I've known Asher Garfinkel for nearly twenty years. He and I were film majors together at Syracuse University. He was a production assistant on my thesis film—and a good one, by the way—before he went on to write and direct an accomplished student film of his own. His passion for film was only matched by his generous spirit and positive energy. Over the years our respective lives took us in different directions, but we stayed in touch.

I was nonetheless surprised and honored when he asked me to write the foreword to his book. What could I possibly have to say about what he had written? When I read the book, however, I realized how much its subject had impacted my career and what a terrific resource it would be for anyone starting out in the business.

Information is king in Hollywood. And coverage is information. It is part of the strategy that gets screenplays sold and movies made. Knowing whether a script received good or bad coverage, or was covered at all, is essential information for writers, producers, and agents as they maneuver to get a script sold.

Good coverage can swing someone's opinion of a script in your favor. It can be sent with the script to a competitive studio to make them believe someone else is already interested and, more importantly, is operating ahead of them. Conversely, existing bad coverage can be obviated by resubmitting the material with a different title and author, hopefully resulting in better coverage and a second chance at a sale.

As you can see, a piece of coverage can be used far beyond the simple analysis of the material itself. Coverage is an integral part of the Hollywood system. Learning to write coverage is an integral part of working in Hollywood.

My second job in the industry was working as a reader at a production company based at Warner Bros. (My first was in the mail room at New Line Cinema.) Although it was a salaried position, there were no benefits. I worked out of my lousy little studio apartment. I was required to write two to three pieces of coverage a day and eight to ten on weekends. I was on call twenty-four hours a day, seven days a week, to do rush coverage on hot scripts that needed immediate consideration. It was a very demanding job. But after hustling mail, answering phones, and ordering copy paper, it was a huge opportunity.

The problem was I had *no idea what I was doing*. I was terrified my secret would be revealed when I delivered my first assignment. To make matters worse, I could find *nothing* in the marketplace that would teach me how to intelligently analyze material and write dependable coverage.

Thankfully, I was blessed with forgiving and kind bosses who apparently saw something in my work, overlooked my lack of experience, and provided strong guidance and criticism as I waded through an enormous amount of material under constant deadlines.

It wasn't until later that I realized how valuable this intense regimen had been. My ability to assess the commercial merit of material had increased dramatically. My capacity to isolate problems in a screenplay and quickly generate creative, in-depth solutions had grown. My writing ability had also sharpened considerably, which translated into story notes that were clear, concise, and thoughtful.

Ultimately, whether doing coverage is a short-term or long-term plan for you, it's a great way to build your storytelling and writing skills. And these skills are essential for many a job in Hollywood—be it as agent, writer, or development executive. Even a good assistant should be able to generate intelligent coverage. Creative, analytical thinking is the cornerstone of this creative business. How you apply this thinking will dictate the course your career takes.

The good news, however, is you won't need to rely on nice bosses to get a solid education in writing coverage. This book will teach you everything and prepare you fully for the job of story analyst as well as much, much more.

Welcome to Hollywood!
Craig Perry
Producer

Craig Perry's producing credits include Universal's *American Pie* franchise; New Line Cinema's *Final Destination* franchise; Warner Bros.' *Cats & Dogs*; Sony Pictures' *The Big Hit* and *Little Black Book*; and Helkon Media's *RepliKate*.

Previously, Perry served as vice president of development for Scott Rudin Productions and director of development for Silver Pictures. He was an associate producer on *The First Wives Club*, and worked on developing such films as *Rules of Engagement, Sleepy Hollow, A Simple Plan, The Truman Show, In & Out, Ransom, Clueless, Twilight, Lethal Weapon 3, Executive Decision, Richie Rich,* and *Demolition Man.*

Introduction

I will never forget. It was September 11, 2001, 8:30 A.M. PST. From what I knew at the moment, our nation was still under full attack, the entire free world was crumbling into ruin . . . *Ring!* It was the phone in my home office. Who could be calling me for business at a devastating time like this? I pried myself from the TV to pick up, and—whaddaya know—it was a client of mine. She was wondering if she could have her screenplay coverage that morning, rather than the afternoon as we had originally agreed. My head was spinning—I had just been contemplating packing my bags and heading for the hills with my pregnant wife. But this client wanted her coverage a little early, on the morning of 9/11. She told me she understood the magnitude of the events unfolding in New York and Washington and that she, too, had just watched the second tower crumble . . . but she also had a film to produce and was desperately relying on this bit of feedback so she could get on with a rewrite. No joke.

I also recall running the story department at a major film company and the many Friday evenings when my colleagues and I would cram into our boss' office for our dreaded weekend reading assignments. In addition to the required reading of our own submissions, we could depend on her dishing everybody a generous mound from *her* script pile—those that she didn't want to touch. We would groan aloud at the thought of spending another weekend on the couch with another serial killer, another femme fatale in a dusty town, another heartless businessman who learns the true meaning of Christmas. In her weekly display of detached sympathy, she would tell us not to sweat it—simply to skim through thirty pages, read the coverage, and let her know what we thought on Monday morning.

I can also tell you about the time when, after months of passionate labor, I completed my own screenplay and sent it to a distant cousin of mine, who was a principal at a major feature film acquisitions house. When I hadn't heard back from her in a couple of weeks, I decided to suck it up and give her a ring. She took my call immediately, which was a boost to my pride and confidence, but when I asked her what she thought about my screenplay, she told me point blank that she just couldn't see it happening at her company, or anywhere for that matter. She then went on to tell me that the *coverage* in front of her called the script a "daring piece," but that it also declared negative *x* about the marketability, negative *y* about the characters, and negative *z* about the tone, and that she really trusted this reader, who had followed her from company to company for twelve years. Unabashedly, she continued reading directly from the comments section of that particular evaluation and then politely excused herself to take a more important call. She never read my script.

Recently, I had a conversation with a Harvard University screenwriting professor. She told me about one of her students who was offered $250,000 for his screenplay. But when the potential buyers got a hold of negative coverage for the script—from the writer's own agency, mind you—they retracted, and the kid never saw a penny.

And then, how could I forget my arrival in L.A. for the first time? Perhaps it will be you soon, or it might have been you, when you took the first few steps into The Business: brimming with optimism, unbridled eagerness to learn, the thirst to make your mark. Almost immediately, I began my job search. While only about one in twenty calls gave me any time of day, those who did elect to chat asked me what kind of scripts I liked to read and requested coverage samples to accompany my résumé. Somehow, I thought, they didn't understand; I had just gotten there. I didn't have "coverage samples," much less know what true professional story analysis looked like. Sure, I had tried my hand at it once in a screenwriting course back in college, but those scraps of paper had long been recycled.

What I did at that point was contact some buddies who had already infiltrated The System and asked them for some examples of coverage. They threw in a couple of screenplays and I began to dabble, unguided, with my own story analysis portfolio. I could not help but feel frustrated that I didn't know this skill coming into it—that I had not been taught coverage in film school or come across it in any publications. For lack of a comprehensive book that encapsulates this Hollywood process, it took a few months to teach myself story analysis and confidently apply again for various internships and assistant positions.

Through all the above experiences—and several unmentioned ones—I have come to acknowledge how truly reliant the entertainment industry is on such a practice as script coverage, sometimes referred to as "story analysis." After conducting a good bit of research on the topic, I was unable to pinpoint the exact origins of script coverage, but Jerry Drucker, who ran the story files department at Paramount Pictures in the 1950s, is convinced that it was used as early as the dawn of the studio era. Jerry recalls: "The story files department had a huge library of index cards, listing authors, cross-referenced titles, loglines, genre of material, and form of submission, for every story coming to the studio. Some of the index cards went back to the silent film era. I recall seeing all three versions of Cecil B. De Mille's *Squaw Man* in the files." (The first *Squaw Man* was filmed in 1914.)

Brian Morewitz, who ran the story department at New Line Cinema, served as senior vice president at Escape Artists, and is now vice president of drama development at ABC Television, says of story analysis today: "Coverage is an institution in the entertainment world, a remarkably influential and useful tool. I have seen it guide executives in their decision-making process, affect project development, and even contribute to the occasional launching of a career."

Hence, the purpose of this book is to offer a reliable resource that explores: 1) the act of reading scripts with a critical mind, 2) the formatting, techniques, and terms involved in professional story analysis, and 3) how to generate paid work through the use of this skill. The aim is to familiarize you in a few sittings with what took me a few years to master.

I should say that some experienced story consultants prefer the sexiness of the phrase "story analysis" versus the cold implications of the word "coverage" and therefore insist that "story analysis" is in a league above "common" script evaluation. To be fair to that camp, one might say that *all coverage is story analysis*, though *all story analysis is not coverage*, given that there exist more in-depth forms of script evaluation, which will be discussed in a later section of this book. Still, for our purposes herein, the two terms will be interchanged.

What Is Coverage, Who Uses It, and Why?

Okay, let us rewind for a moment to address some basics. Remember those book reports you used to write in elementary school? You know: read the book, summarize it, and tell the teacher what you thought about it. Well, coverage is not unlike a book report, except it is used mainly for screenplays. A reader will read a screenplay, type up a general cover page with his overall take on the material, and then create a one- to two-page synopsis of the story as well as one to two pages of comments about its strengths, weaknesses, and potential in the marketplace.

Coverage is widely used and accepted in Hollywood for the process called *development*, which could be defined as any or all steps taken to move a story idea into the actual production phase of that project. This development process can originate with a simple idea, a short outline, a verbal pitch, a magazine article, a book, a play, a comic book, a graphic novel, a treatment (an extensive outline for a screenplay), a preexisting film or TV show, a video game, or a screenplay itself. Development involves all efforts to acquire or arrive at a final draft of a screenplay in addition to the pursuit of talent, above-the-line crew (i.e., directors, writers, and producers), and, ultimately, financing to turn that script into celluloid reality.

Barring some technical production and post-production crew ("below-the-line"), almost everyone in the film industry is in some way involved in or touched by development. Producers, actors, agents, managers, writers, directors, studio execs and sometimes editors, cinematographers, composers, and special effects people, as well as any support staff associated with this list are all looking for that next fabulous idea to boost their own careers. When they find it they will all be talking to each other (or trying to or hoping to) in an attempt to move this story idea, in whatever form, from the page to the screen. And as that story circulates from one expert, one level, and one company to another, you can bet it will be covered by various professional readers several times.

During the development process, a company or individual may have a screenplay analyzed for one of various reasons—the most common being a *gatekeeping* function, to sift through the sheer volumes of story submissions one might receive on a weekly basis. As an illustration, let's make up a company, Flag Films, which might consist of any combination of the professionals mentioned above. It's a fictitious entity, but the following numbers are quite possible:

Let's say Flag Films receives twenty screenplay submissions a week. On average, it takes an individual about one and a half hours to read a decent, readable screenplay. That means that Flag Films would have to assign a minimum of thirty in-house staff hours per week to simply reading and analyzing the screenplays that fill its mailbox. Is the CEO of the company going to sort through them all for thirty hours? Or the VP of production and development? Or any other executive or manager? Some would say they should, but Flag Films might only employ three or four full-time employees—that's thirty staff hours when a company needs those same hours to be out there looking for the next best thing, putting together financing, cultivating relationships, developing in-house projects, and seeing them through production, in addition to day-to-day operations. Why spend all that time searching for a needle in a haystack when roughly 98 percent of those submissions, in the opinion of any reader, sadly will not surpass the worth of the dust on their shelves?

Often a company such as our Flag Films will have assistants and/or interns do the gatekeeping for them and sort out the truly bad material and push the small handful of promising ones up a step in the development ladder. After their read, this support staff will probably be required to show their employers a summary of the story and their thoughts in the form of coverage. Many other companies hire freelance story analysts and pay them for coverage on a per-script basis. Others outsource their story department with a coverage service that will take care of their script reading in bulk (such as my own Readers Unlimited, pardon the plug). Wealthy studios such as 20th Century Fox who might receive more than five thousand submissions annually, have full-time, in-house, union readers set up in trailers right there on the lot.

To wade through an overwhelming number of submissions is not the only reason to employ story analysts. Sometimes a company or individual might simply require objective, reliable *feedback* on a single script. A writer, for example, may have worked on her screenplay for so long that she has lost sight of the strengths and weaknesses of her property. Before taking that once-in-a-lifetime chance to submit a script to a golden contact, she might want to make sure it is up to snuff. Or, a producer may have paid a writer for a new draft of a script and needs a fresh opinion on that project in its latest form. A director may be about to commit to a certain project but needs that extra affirmation from an outside mind that this is the right thing to pursue.

Coverage can also provide *information* to industry professionals. I was interested to learn that a friend of mine who was on the marketing staff at Sony contacted that studio's story department for coverage on *Spiderman II*, months in advance of its release, as an introduction to the story and nature of the project. Casting directors might rely on coverage as a planning tool, since one will often find character descriptions and, at times, a formal character breakdown within the report.

Still, there is a fourth use for coverage in the development world: it can serve as a *sales* tool. An agent, for example, might want to woo a prospective buyer or other elements toward a certain screenplay. A producer might have partial financing in place for a certain project but still needs the balance from other investors. A director might want to bring certain talent on board a project that she believes in. In which cases, these individuals might mention or share positive coverage of the material with interested parties. When I worked at a studio, I came across situations in which people would use positive coverage to sell a certain project internally, that is, to their superior(s), in order to help sway their opinion in favor of that property.

Why Learn How to Read Scripts and Write Coverage?

Certainly, if you would like to make a living as a credible professional reader, this book is for you. But there are other reasons to learn story analysis. I urge you to read on if one or more of the following applies to you:

1. *You wish to become more marketable in your search for an entry-level post.* Whether applying for an internship or assistant position, be assured that someone who has written coverage before is far more likely to be considered and

hired than someone who has not. One who can effectively screen submissions and provide feedback on company projects—verbally or in writing—brings far more value to the interview than one who cannot.

2. *If you have surpassed entry-level work, reading and understanding the essentials of script evaluation will be helpful for further production and development jobs.* John Cheng is head of feature development for Brett Ratner's Rat Entertainment (*Rush Hour, Rush Hour 2, Family Man, X-Men: The Last Stand*) and co-producer of New Line Cinema's *Horrible Bosses* and *Code Name: The Cleaner.* He shares: "It's important for aspiring executives to learn how to write coverage, because it's a great way to practice identifying the key points to the plot and to learn how to articulate your comments in a concise, clear manner." As you climb toward becoming a producer, director, agent, or development executive, you will inevitably be in a position where you are asked to sort through volumes of submissions and provide feedback on in-house projects, either verbally or in writing. At some point in your life you might even have to hire and supervise readers yourself. Before you start seeking able readers or start critiquing your readers' work, you should know how to capably read and report on a script yourself. After knowledgably reading a hundred or so scripts, you will begin to grasp what works, what doesn't, and what trends are out there.

3. *You might be a screenwriter who intends to submit your material somewhere for consideration.* Then, it is a case of "knowing your enemy," that is, the person who will be evaluating your script. Reading and analyzing other people's scripts will make an invaluable contribution to your own screenwriting skills. By learning story analysis, you will come to know what they're looking for out there and how to earn points in an objective reader's mind.

4. *Interested in becoming a film critic?* Granted, writing for a newspaper or magazine represents a different angle and craft, since you will be analyzing the finished product (including cinematography, acting, soundtrack, production design, etc.). But there is considerable overlap between film critique and coverage when picking apart the story elements of a completed film. Did you ever see a film review that did not mention story or screenplay?

5. *If you are a writing instructor, you are probably well versed in the art of screenwriting, but you might be less so in the weight that story analysis carries within the industry and the technique that goes into it.* Alternatively, you might know the value and craft of coverage but have found yourself with little time to teach it to your students during a crammed semester.

6. *If you are reading this, chances are you would like to make money through some facet of the entertainment industry.* But there may be a few out there who are simply intrigued souls who would like to know a little more about what's behind the trusted gatekeeping system of story analysis. To you folks, I say keep reading. After examining the nuts, bolts, and business of coverage, you will never look at another screenplay, movie, or novel the same way again.

I should declare up front that this is not a how-to book on screenwriting or on the business of screenwriting. Naturally, we will have to cover many of the basic elements you would find in a screenwriting book, but I will do so in much less detail, within only the first section of three in this book (Section I: What's in a Screenplay?). In fact, to supplement this section, I urge you to read a few screenwriting books and take classes or workshops, which will offer you a firm understanding of what goes into constructing the very works that you are about to learn how to dissect. There are additional titles listed in Appendix B, but a few publications I believe to be exceptional are:

Write Screenplays That Sell: The Ackerman Way, by Hal Ackerman

The Writer's Journey: Mythic Structure For Storytellers & Screenwriters, by Christopher Vogler

Making a Good Script Great, by Linda Seger

Screenwriting: The Art, Craft and Business of Film and Television Writing, by Richard Walter

Screenwriting Is Storytelling: Creating an A-List Screenplay That Sells, by Kate Wright

Section II: What's in Coverage? will build upon the knowledge and intuition that you glean from the first section of this book and help you to put them to use to create a story analyst's report. It is a highly practical and comprehensive look at all the details and thought that go into standard coverage, from the title of the submission down to the recommendation of the material and writer.

Section III: The Business will remind you that story analysis is not for those who are in search of that glamorous life or artistic career in a golden Hollywood utopia. Rather, script coverage represents the gritty front lines of story development; it is first and foremost a business. In Section III, I will share my fifteen years of wisdom on the topic with useful guidelines for practicing, developing your portfolio, getting the work, and then maintaining it.

In conjunction with your own abilities, talents, drive, and instincts, these sections will empower you to turn your knowledge into constructive, career-building strides within the film and television industry.

SECTION I
What's in a Screenplay?

TERMS, TECHNIQUES, AND GENERAL STORY ELEMENTS YOU MUST KNOW BEFORE EVALUATING A SCREENPLAY

S o, you are handed your first script to read as an industry professional. Within a given set of specs, you will be required to summarize the story and then comment on it clearly, intelligently, and objectively, either verbally or in writing. Of course you have your personal tastes, and you can and should share your gut reaction in the comments you prepare. But you will also have to be able to discuss *why*, above those initial likes and dislikes, the material works or does not as a piece of writing for the screen.

While you are reading a screenplay or teleplay, keep in mind that there is a widely accepted set of rules and a lingo that your employer (or client, depending on how they're paying you; more about the business in Section III) will expect you to reference when detailing your thoughts about that material. It is essential that you become well versed in the following storytelling basics before you can declare yourself ready to critique a screenplay. At times, these elements may feel surprisingly cut-and-dried, considering they relate to the evaluation of a piece of fiction. While your instincts will eventually come into play as much as "the rules" (and we will discuss the issue of subjectivity in a later section), these fundamentals will provide a solid foundation.

As mentioned in the introduction, our objective is not to learn how to *write* these elements into a script so much as how to *recognize* and *evaluate* them. Nonetheless, both angles require that you familiarize yourself with these fundamentals. There are myriad screenwriting books, workshops, and classes that delve into these elements in great detail and that provide extensive examples. Consider the pages of this section to be a quick refresher on those widely embraced teaching tools. Along the way, I will place in **boldface** many of the terms that are frequently used in coverage and development circles. They should become a part of your critiquing vocabulary.

1

Plot

If you were completing a complex jigsaw puzzle, you would probably start by identifying the largest and most obvious pieces and then build outward (or inward) from there. In a lot of ways, a screenplay resembles such a puzzle. Naturally, for a screenplay to achieve a satisfying whole, several smaller pieces must connect or interlock with the more prominent ones, but there are three main pieces with which one can begin: plot, structure, and character.

The first piece, **plot** (sometimes referred to as **storyline** or **narrative** by readers), is simply the string of events, actions, and reactions revolving around the main story portrayed in a script. If the script is essentially about a scientific team who defends the Earth from an onslaught of human-eating tomatoes, then every event, revelation, or progression that takes place in the story and revolves around this main idea is the plot. A strong plot will adhere to what is often described as the **central conflict, throughline**, or **narrative spine** of a script, which stems from the protagonist's pursuit of a primary, tangible goal and the main opposing force working against him or her.

It must be noted that sometimes people confuse plot with **Story**. Plot is what the script is about, though usually on a more superficial level. Story, however, can go a step further to cover deeper layers of theme and character. If someone asks you what the script is about, they probably do want to know the essence of its plot. But if they go on to correct you and ask you what it's *about*, they probably want the Story, or a sense of the author's underlying intentions. For example, *Big Fish* might be regarded as a story about a dying man's recollection of some magical experiences during his youth. But then the Story is truly *about* a father and son trying to connect on common ground before it is too late. *School of Rock* is about a slovenly rocker wannabe who poses as a substitute teacher and enlists his young students into the band of his dreams, though it's *about* growing up, personal responsibility, knowing one's limitations, and tapping into one's potential.

A good plot will challenge a hero through a rigorous test of action and reaction resulting in a pattern of two steps forward/one or more back. For those sports buffs out there, this analogy might work for you (and for those of you who don't care for American football, please bear with me): A hero starts the story on his own goal line and, to win the "game," he must work the length of the field within a very short timeframe. A forward pass or run might provide some significant yardage, but a sack, botched play, or incompletion can just as easily negate those accomplishments, along with the constant risk of fumble or interception. An offense will have a general plan and a tangible goal, but along the way it must adjust each play to survive those surprises and pitfalls it encounters.

Good plots also offer the viewer/reader mounds of **conflict**. Conflict means two opposing forces clashing, and it is conflict that constitutes **drama**, the stuff that engages an audience. Without conflict, nothing would happen in a story. Years ago, a screenwriting professor told our class that a good script will present conflict in *every scene* and on *every page*. Through my years of professional reading, I have held these words sacred (and have since heard them out of the mouths of several other gurus) as a crucial litmus test when evaluating a screenplay. The more conflict the better. It can take the form of hero versus human, hero versus nature, hero versus himself, technology, an idea, or anything else a writer might dream up.

While a plot is built around the idea of one central conflict, adversity can also arise out of a smaller **complication** within the plot. A complication is simply the introduction of an obstacle or bump (extra conflict) in the protagonist's path as he attempts to get from point A to B. This setback can be as large as an army of thousands or as simple as a hangnail. It will usually delay the hero on his journey, either imminently or down the road. A **reversal**, on the other hand, is quite often a significant complication for the protagonist—one that sends the entire plot and list of characters hurtling in a new direction. As audience members and readers, we love reversals, because they change up the pace and backdrop of a script. A reversal might also be labeled a **twist**, especially if it's an event or revelation that completely upends the reality we have thought to exist until that moment.

Who could forget the famous twist in *The Crying Game*? Fergus (played by Stephen Rea) has fled to London from Ireland after botching his hostage execution. There, he finds anonymity and eventually becomes intimate with his deceased hostage's girlfriend, Dil (Jaye Davidson). After Dil reveals herself to be a man, Fergus spends much of the rest of the film reconciling his disgust with his innate need to do what is right and his deep feelings for Dil as a person. In *The Italian Job*, a humongous reversal unfolds when Stella (Charlize Theron) inadvertently reveals to Steve (Edward Norton) that she is the daughter of John Bridger (Donald Sutherland). Playing the cable girl as she aims for information and distraction, Stella lets one of her father's isms ("the Devil inside") slip while they are on a dinner date. Steve suddenly makes the connection, the heist team's cover is blown, and they are left to adjust their entire game plan for the remainder of the story.

A reversal, however, need not always be a complication. It might actually be a revelation or development that benefits the protagonist during his struggle and propels him forward on his journey in an unexpected way. Consider *Finding Nemo*, in which we begin to think it's the end of the line for Marlin, who is a bit lost after having come so far and then gets swallowed by a whale. But in a fortuitous reversal, the whale does the unexpected by shooting Marlin through his blowhole and into the waters of Sydney's bay, thus putting the little fish back on track in his quest to find his son.

As a critical reader, you will also be sensitive to weaknesses in plot called **plot holes**. A plot hole is a gap or disconnect in information that leaves an audience/reader wondering how a certain character deduced something or how a character physically arrived at one place from another. As an exaggerated example, if we see a character in jail in one scene and the next time we see him he is roaming the streets in a clown outfit—without our ever having received dialogue or visual about how he got to this point—that is a plot hole. If a character loves his girlfriend in one scene and slams the door in her face for cheating on him in the next—without our ever learning how he came to this point—that is also a plot hole.

However, a piece of writing may take its time in revealing important bits of information or a writer may choose to leave certain things vague during a film or at its conclusion. At the very end of *Unfaithful*, Connie (Diane Lane) and Ed (Richard Gere) arrive at an intersection, literally and symbolically. Here, they could either flee, with the hopes of finding a new life, or Ed could turn himself in at the police station that looms some thirty feet away from them. In *Garden State*, Andrew (Zach Braff) opts not to head back to Los Angeles so quickly after all, instead reuniting with Sam (Natalie Portman) in the airport where they agree that their relationship is crazy, but they'll take it a day at a time to see how it goes. Rather than the predominant "happily-ever-after" approach, such open-endedness is acceptable technique meant to leave you wondering or thinking for yourself. It can only be categorized as a hole if—given all information by the end of the story—the actual narrative still does not make logical sense.

Subplot

A well-written plot will be accompanied by **subplot**—actually, an average of two to six of them. While subplots usually take stories on a quick detour away from their main storylines, a good writer will make sure that each subplot is spawned by, intersects with, and/or is resolved by the main plot throughout the piece. A subplot may even serve as a complication in the plot.

As an example, in *Raiders of the Lost Ark*, the *plot*, or the central conflict, is about an archaeologist who is trying to acquire the Ark of the Covenant before it falls into the hands of the Nazis, but the main *subplot* is the relationship between Indy and Marian. This relationship, however, does not rest on a separate track from the plot. Instead, the Indy–Marian subplot unfolds *as a result of* events in the plot and the subplot sometimes influences the next step in the story. In order for Indy to pursue the Ark, he must begrudgingly allow Marian to accompany him, since she insists on hanging onto a big piece of the puzzle, the medallion that will complete the Staff of Ra. Thus, a subplot is born. Only through their subsequent pursuit of the Ark do Indy and Marian gradually allow their feelings for each other to emerge.

The narrative spine of *The Full Monty* is clearly about a group of down-and-out steelworkers who decide to model an act after the Chippendales in order to make some quick cash, but the story is also rich with subplot. Gaz (Robert Carlyle) struggles to recover some respect in the eyes of his son and ex-wife; low on self-esteem, "Big Dave" (Mark Addy) fears intimacy with his wife, not to mention exposing his fat body to the world; Gerald (Tom Wilkinson) attempts to get his career back on track while trying to keep his unemployed status a secret from his oblivious wife. The central conflict drives and inspires each of these "B" storylines, while complications in the subplots often affect the entire group in pursuit of their main goal.

Subplot can give the story a chance to breathe and infuse the plot with emotion. It allows characters to sit back from the central conflict and reflect on their experiences along the way. It can also serve as a source of **theme** in the story. In *The Full Monty*, Dave realizes by the end that his wife and others love him for who he is. Pushing Gerald to go through with their extravagant plan, Gaz tells him that he has the rest of his life to wear a suit. Both of these concepts represent themes generated by subplot. More about theme a little later.

Backstory

One other element of plot to be considered is **backstory**, which is essentially an event or events that are relevant to the story and/or characters but have taken place *before* the actual timeline of the script begins. We usually learn about backstory through dialogue, though it might also be revealed through a news report, a piece of writing, a dream sequence, a flashback, voiceover, or any other way you can imagine. For example, an innovative method of backstory revelation unfolds in *Ice Age*, as Manfred (the woolly mammoth) observes some cave hieroglyphics that come to life to unveil his history—all without words.

With your knowledge of complications and twists, subplot, backstory, and the other plot essentials, you will be ready to place that first large puzzle piece firmly on the table. Still, when reading scripts, it is imperative that you be able to identify and evaluate two other segments that carry equal weight: structure and character.

2

Structure

Structure is considered one of the foremost elements to bear in mind when both writing and evaluating a screenplay. Screenwriting professors will often teach structure before anything else, and chances are, one of the first things your employer will wonder is if the structure of the script you just read is *tight*. Structure is the framework or skeleton upon which plots, subplots, character, and story pace are built. If the structure fails in a screenplay, everything else will likely come crashing down around it. A well-structured script, however, might be considered salvageable even if other layers aren't quite working yet.

The practice of **three-act structure** is, hands down, the most preferred template for screenplay writing and critique alike. Everyone from CEOs to development execs to screenwriting gurus will tell you that any story that has survived the ages has been told via a three-act structure. That is not to say that *Hamlet* is a play with only three official acts, but it does work within a framework of a beginning (**ACT I**), middle (**ACT II**), and end (**ACT III**), which some gurus have also called the **setup, development**, and **conclusion.**

When asked why there are three acts, many experts will tell you, "Because that's the way it's always been done, dating back to Aristotle," or that three acts have somehow become universally satisfying to the collective unconscious. Few, however, go on to explore *why* it has always been done that way and *why* we find it so satisfying. Perhaps it is because any one act presented alone would feel more like a dry statement than an engaging story. Here are a couple of examples, the first of which is for you skiers:

1. I went to the top of my first triple-black-diamond slope.

To say just that and move on would present an incomplete picture. What if I go on to say:

2. I finally made it down alive, though I'm not sure I'll ever ski one of those again.

Okay, that's how it ended. Now we're getting somewhere, but, when described separately or even juxtaposed, the steps still are not all that interesting. The story is missing a middle—its meat, its heart. So, try this on for size:

1. I went to the top of my first triple-black-diamond slope.

2. On my way down, I fell five times, bumped my head on an icy mogul, lost a mitten and a ski, had to detangle myself from a tree, and resolved to crawl the final quarter of the way to the bottom.

3. I finally made it down alive, though I'm not sure I'll ever ski one of those again.

Can you see how those three in order begin to provide some satisfaction by taking on the form of a story? Another example for you writers:

1. I decided to attempt to write my first screenplay.

Yeah, and . . .?

2. The process turned out not to be as easy as I thought: I lost sleep, pulled out hair, broke up with my girlfriend,

started smoking again, and neglected to feed the cat while navigating the maddening intricacies of writing a complete story for the screen.

Okay, but did you . . .?

3. Through my discipline and heartache I was able to finish the script. It didn't sell, but I am now confident that I can and will continue to write more.

You may or may not buy this logic, but for our purposes here, let's at least agree that: 1) the overwhelming majority of successful scripts has been written utilizing the three-act model, which employs a set beginning, middle, and end, and 2) the universal lingo with which to evaluate screenplay structure employs references to Acts I, II, and III.

The following is a glance at typical three-act structure. As you read, you will note that structure and **character development** go hand in hand. Below, however, I will emphasize structure and its relation to plot, while we will go deeper into character work in the next chapter.

The Three Acts

While a screenplay can vary in page length from about 100 to 135 pages, a count of 120 is considered to be the standard when discussing structure. Think one page per one minute of screen time.

It is taught that **ACT I** kicks off inside a character's (or characters') everyday life. In *The Writer's Journey*, Christopher Vogler, drawing from Joseph Campbell's work, calls it the "Ordinary World," while Linda Seger (*Making a Good Script Great*) simply calls it the "set up." Essentially, we are introduced to the protagonist(s) in a reality that he has known for a good while—that is, a specific state of mind, geography, health, wealth, career, attitude, and/or otherwise. But soon—knowingly or unknowingly—our hero will cross paths with an **inciting incident** or will be delivered a certain **call to adventure,** as Vogler calls it. Here, we are teased, tickled, nudged, warned, or slightly intrigued by the approach of a new force, element, or drive in the main character's life. Such a **catalyst** or **hook** is typically introduced within the first ten pages of the story. Nowadays, to draw audiences in and immediately entertain, you will often find a script with its catalyst at the very opening of the story, such as a murder scene, a chase sequence, a heist, or a fight. This moment or sequence is sometimes referred to as a **teaser**, which is especially common in the one-hour TV format of storytelling.

Over the remainder of the first act, we will get to know our hero for his weaknesses, strengths, likes, dislikes, hopes, history, dreams, talents, and fears, and dark clouds of conflict will brew within his reality, and he may be pushed, poked, prodded, and have to wrestle internally before a specific moment or moments will ultimately shove or attract him into completely new territory. Such a moment is popularly called the **first turning point** (coined by Linda Seger) or **plot point** (coined by Syd Field in his book, *Screenplay*). Since it arrives at the conclusion of Act I, hopefully somewhere between pages twenty and forty, it might also be called **turning point 1** or **plot point 1**. It is essentially one of three main reversals we find in a well-written screenplay.

At this plot point, a situation reaches critical mass for our hero, and he reaches a colossal crossroads in his life or things get too personal for him not to react. Here, the protagonist(s) may choose to dive into a dangerous or uncomfortable new era or he may be pulled into it through no choice of his own. Regardless, he has crossed into a new reality and the heart of the story, called **ACT II.**

Many authors do a fine job of setting up their story in Act I, but it is in the approximate sixty-page **second act** where work can fall apart. Indeed, as tricky as the second act is for the protagonist, a writer has similarly entered a precarious zone. In Act II, along with a host of subplots, writers must assemble a series of complications and reversals and accompanying reactions and recoveries while remaining tethered and true to the central conflict of the plot, the learning curve of the main character, and the overall interest level of the audience/reader. Far easier said than done.

In the first part of the second act, a hero will meet new allies and enemies—some of whom could flip-flop along the way—while getting acclimated to this dangerous new realm. A hero will often begin the second act at a significantly low point (e.g., just escaped from a prison bus wreck with nowhere to go, as in *The Fugitive*) or at a relatively high point (e.g., suddenly endowed with awesome power, as in *Bruce Almighty*). Then, the first half of the second act (call it IIA) will usually head in one of two directions. The hero might spend much of this segment attempting to crawl up and out of a hole so that he improves his situation or status as the act progresses. Conversely, his overall condition could gradually slip as IIA unfolds.

In either scenario, IIA is heading toward the script's **midpoint**, which often presents a major new complication or, better yet, an all-out reversal. Numerically speaking, "midpoint" needn't be taken all that literally. If a script is 120 pages, as a critical reader, you should expect the midpoint to enter the picture anywhere between pages fifty-five and seventy-five. (The aforementioned twist in *The Crying Game*, for example, could be viewed as a midpoint, though it doesn't occur until more than sixty minutes into the film, well over halfway through.) Nor does a midpoint need to occur within one moment, page, or scene. It might occur within a **sequence**, which is a string of scenes and images that are linked to form one idea, such as a chase sequence, a dream sequence, wedding sequence, heist sequence, or a romantic sequence. If you wish to stretch it, you might even consider the entire twenty-minute road trip in the middle of *About Schmidt* to be that film's midpoint.

A midpoint is a crucial structural element. As viewers and readers, we truly rely on it to remain engaged in the story. A midpoint can refresh the plot, renew character resolve, mix up the pace, and/or reemphasize what's at stake for our hero. It presents a major high, a major low, or a quick combination of both in the plotline. In romances and romantic comedies, it might be the first time we see our heroes lock lips or have sex. Often a midpoint will deposit the protagonist into rock bottom, or a pitfall so deep that he finds himself nearly back to square one. It might take our hero uncomfortably close to the death of his cause or even the end of his life.

At the midpoint of *The Village*, Lucius (Joaquin Phoenix) is stabbed by Noah (Adrien Brody), which changes the direction and focus of the story. Suddenly, Ivy (Bryce Dallas Howard) is inspired to head through the forbidden woods herself in search of medicine for Lucius. *The Incredibles* reaches its midpoint when Mr. Incredible: 1) learns about Syndrome's plans to attack his city with a robot and 2) is captured. Suddenly, with Mr. Incredible now a prisoner, the story takes on a new direction; he isn't free to sneak around the island anymore while his family makes their way to investigate his disappearance. In *Hustle & Flow*, Djay and his crew stumble across the "hook" that will push their song over the top: "It's hard out here for a pimp." The momentum created by that midpoint breakthrough carries these characters and their story for the rest of the act.

The remainder of the second act (call it IIB) will then be spun as a reaction to the midpoint. With new knowledge, wounds, power, allies, enemies, or deficiencies, the main character of a well-structured script will emerge from this deep, dark (or wholly enlightened) place and head in a direction we probably never would have imagined in the beginning. If up to now, the lead character has mainly been passive, it is time for him to step up and make things happen in the story. If up to this point, the character has mainly pursued a superficial goal, we might begin to see signs of his looking inward. During IIB, this hero may follow a new lead or instinct, pick up clues from unexpected places, slide into deeper trouble, and certainly face a host of unexpected new complications as he scrambles to get back on track toward the goal he set at the beginning of the act. All of this will culminate with the protagonist's lowest point, which is often called **turning point 2** or **plot point 2**. This moment or segment usually features another prominent reversal and should fall approximately sixty pages (think screen minutes) after the first act break.

Some, such as Robert McKee, have also labeled this turning point the "Act II climax," while I have heard others refer to it as the "low point," and rightly so, as this is where all events of the second act come to a head, all information is laid on the table, and the protagonist's aims usually come crashing down. Here, we often find a character who has gone quite a distance against many odds, and, weary as he may be, has overcome personal flaws and fears and is finally informed, enlightened, resolved, or healed enough to face his greatest enemy. Similar to the first act break and the midpoint, this final turning point of the script propels the story into yet another playing field, raises new questions, further emphasizes old ones, or recommits the hero to his cause. A good second plot point usually generates enough momentum or intensity to carry a story through **ACT III** to the script's conclusion.

In the third act, our hero might go after his antagonist, or he might let the antagonist come to him. Regardless, at this point, the hero is so close to having achieved his goals that he can almost taste the rewards (and so can we). But first, he'll have to fight that last battle—internally, externally, or both. That "battle" is the main event of the entire story and it may be laid out as one long sequence. Writers try to keep their third act intriguing, suspenseful, horrifying, humorous, and/or emotional by ratcheting up the risks a protagonist must take—often within a given amount of time (see more about **urgency** in chapter 4).

Sometimes Act III portrays a hero diving back into the "hornets' nest," which he knows to be lethal. He's already been there, but must return to take care of unfinished business. Around the midpoint of *Training Day*, Jake (Ethan Hawke) and Alonzo (Denzel Washington) head into "The Jungle," a nasty enclave of violence and crime in South Los Angeles where Alonzo happens to be keeping a girlfriend and his young son. Alonzo warns Jake not to ever go there without him. When things go awry, Jake seeks revenge and justice for Alonzo's various betrayals, so the rookie walks right back into "The Jungle" to confront his former mentor, hence his darkest fears. Likewise, in *Star Wars*, Luke has already been in the heart of the Empire once and witnessed the damage that Vader can do, yet in Act III, he chooses to accompany the Rebels to the center of the Death Star in order to destroy it.

Subsequently, the hero will be exposed to a near-death situation, which might mean literal near-death, though it also could signify a brush with the "death" or loss of everything this character stands or hopes for, such as the loss of love, loss of self-esteem, loss of a cause. This near-death moment, experienced when face to face with the hero's worst fear or enemy, is considered to be the **climax** and usually hits within one to five pages of the end of the script. A climax can take the form of a sentence, monologue, scene, or sequence.

In 99 percent of all scripts, the hero will cull every last ounce of strength and gram of knowledge or wisdom to overcome this potentially fatal climax, after which, we'll get a dose of **resolution** or **denouement**. The resolution of most tightly structured scripts will only last a few pages, maximum. It will answer all questions, tie up most or all loose ends, complete every character, let us take one more breath in this world, perhaps laugh or cry with our hero for one more instant, and then firmly say, "The End," in a satisfying way. A poorly structured script, on the other hand, will drag out the resolution for a number of pages. Having witnessed the climax, a reader will be ready to close the pages and fully assess the material, only to have the author insist on hanging on for extended conversation or information that seems irrelevant to the plot.

Likewise, strong subplots will follow their own beginning-middle-end template. The rules for subplots aren't so rigid, however, as they are for the plot. You may find the setup of a subplot at the very beginning of a script, but a subplot may not even start until after the midpoint. Additionally, the major beats inherent to each act (e.g., inciting incident, turning points, climax) needn't be as pronounced. Regardless, through subplot, a writer is telling a mini-drama—a story within the framework of a larger story that is only likely to satisfy if it defines its own three acts.

Other Structural Considerations

While reading, you might come across some material that seems **episodic** within its second act. An episodic structure isn't necessarily good or bad, but as an active reader, you should be able to identify it. To say episodic means that we are given a string of chronologically compartmentalized subplots that may serve to develop and/or hinder the hero but are otherwise unrelated to one another. A classic episodic tale is *The Odyssey*, in which Ulysses embarks on his journey, bouncing from locale to locale, making different friends and battling different enemies. Each situation or character has little to do with the others, other than to have touched Ulysses in some way on his journey.

Road movies are often in danger of becoming overly episodic, especially if the characters, information, tools, and obstacles encountered during one detour don't ever return to the plot later. While *The Straight Story* has its virtues, some might argue that it plays a bit slow as Alvin (Richard Farnsworth) goes from point to loosely connected point. *Apocalypse Now* could be considered episodic in its second act. As the heroes journey up river, they grow (or perish) only via a series of relatively unrelated pit stops. *Transamerica*, too, is an episodic tale, given that Bree (Felicity Huffman) and Toby (Kevin Zegers) make various unlinked pit stops en route to California.

Most scripts are structured chronologically, but you might come across a small handful that take a more **nonlinear** approach. Quentin Tarantino has proven to be a master at such technique, structuring *Pulp Fiction* and *Kill Bill* out of sequential time. *Memento*, written in reverse chronology, seems to have shunned all structural binds. Other nonlinear examples are *Run Lola Run, Eternal Sunshine of the Spotless Mind*, and *The Limey*. Yet, if you study these relatively unconventional films a little more closely, you might be able to pick out a sense of the setup, conflict development, and resolution phases in each of them, the same as in any other three-act framework. *Memento*, for example, is told in complete reverse order, yet three acts are still intrinsic to this seemingly atypical storyline.

Memento: A Study of Nonlinear Substructure and How the Three Acts Emerge
Act I

Leonard kills Teddy at an empty, secluded shack in the desert, insisting that Teddy is John G. We get to know Leonard and learn that he has a "special condition" that affects his memory and that he is after someone dangerous named John G, who killed his wife. He used to be an insurance adjuster and now he spends his days driven by revenge.

Turning point 1: We see Leonard spending time with both Natalie and Teddy, both of whom seem to be instrumental in his ongoing investigation.

Act II

We find Leonard sunken into the quagmire of his investigation, with Natalie joining him as his ally. Leonard is intensely suspicious of this guy Teddy, whose name actually happens to be John Gammell. He has even written a note to himself on Teddy's picture not to trust him. We also see that Leonard has someone captive in his closet by the name of Dodd and we begin to wonder if he is the key to uncovering who this John G is.

Midpoint: A new threat accosts Leonard in the way of this mysterious Dodd, an incensed stranger with a gun. For the rest of Act II, we learn that Dodd is connected to Natalie, who appears to be in some distress, while Teddy implores Leonard to get off his current track with this woman.

Turning point 2: Here, we learn that Natalie's been using Leonard's disability and his obsession with revenge from the beginning to take out Dodd (her deceased boyfriend's drug-dealing partner) and ultimately Teddy.

Act III

We watch Natalie lure Leonard and see that Teddy is actually "the cop" with whom he's been speaking during the chain of black-and-white scene interludes. Teddy's clues direct Leonard to an empty, secluded shack in the desert, where he kills Jimmy Grants, Natalie's boyfriend.

Climax: Teddy shows up to reveal that he was the cop who helped Leonard track down and kill the real John G a year ago and, while he's been using him to deal with his own slate of criminals, he's also been giving Leonard purpose and hope to an otherwise pointless existence. Leonard refuses to accept the truth and scribbles "Don't trust him" on Teddy's Polaroid image, only to begin his aimless search for the next John G.

Memento
(2000, Newmarket Films, Columbia TriStar Home Video)
Screenplay by Christopher Nolan
Based on a short story by Jonathan Nolan
Directed by Christopher Nolan

Effectively written plot and structure will provide you, the reader, with the roads and a map. Still, your experience will seem hollow without someone to guide you through the proposed journey. Bring in the characters.

3

Character

Characters supply heart, soul, dimension, direction, emotion, message, and universal appeal to a story. When one mentions character, the first type that will probably come to mind is the **hero** or **protagonist**, whom we've already focused on quite a bit. A good story will paint the essence of this main character within the first act and then rock his everyday world by the first turning point, sending him on the journey of a lifetime and to places internally and/or externally that he had never imagined. The events of the second and third acts should represent the most defining, taxing, significant moments of a character's life. This is either the first story he would tell his grandchildren, or it's the one he would swear never to tell.

The Hero

In the first act of a script, we usually find our hero with both **wants** and **needs**. There is something that person might want (e.g., a briefcase full of cash, true love, revenge, any main goal that drives the plot) but isn't aware of what he actually *needs* (e.g., to realize that money isn't everything, to be more comfortable in his own shoes, to let go of an obsession). For the remainder of the story, the hero should undergo a gradual transformation toward satisfying that need, which is induced by the plot, structure, and other characters. Such change is frequently called **character arc**. In *School of Rock*, Dewey (Jack Black) begins the story in a lazy, delusional state but learns by the end that, while his original dreams will never come true, he can still be fulfilled if he directs some energy toward teaching kids. That transformation from freeloading slob to responsible, happy adult is his arc. In *Jerry Maguire*, we watch Jerry (Tom Cruise) move from a loveless "bottom feeder" to one who opens himself to emotional connection. Without character arc, a story could seem stagnant and devoid of purpose.

The core message or theme of the film often derives from the character's transformation. In the case of *School of Rock*, the obvious theme that emerges is as the Rolling Stones might put it: "You can't always get what you want, but if you try sometimes [and accept some responsibility] you get what you need." Through *Jerry Maguire*, we are told that life is empty and difficult without someone to share it with. Often at the midpoint of the script, we will find the main character as close to the completion point of his arc as he is to the state in which he began his journey.

A good protagonist should also be accessible to a reader/audience. Not that everyone knows what it's like to be a Navy fighter pilot, but we do know what it is to have hopes, dreams, beliefs, fears, flaws, hobbies, habits, secrets, and emotions. The combination of these elements within one character will create **dimension**, making him seem more human and therefore more real or "fleshed out." The inclusion of such details about a character, in tandem with his arc, might be referred to as **character development**. Such information will be relayed via what the character says, what others say about him, what the character does, and how he reacts to both mundane and extreme situations. In *When Harry Met Sally*, for example, Sally's meticulous, if difficult, manner of ordering food in a restaurant tells us a lot about this picky woman who is trying to maintain control in her life. This idiosyncrasy does little for the movement of the plot, but evidence of her likes and dislikes makes her more real.

A real character should also come across as **complex**. There are very few people in the world who could ever be categorized as 100 percent good or 100 percent evil. Rather, we all have several layers of weakness, hate, strength, and love within us. The best protagonists are often painted with dimension by the exploration of such human complexities, especially in dramatic pieces. In *Mystic River*, for example, we get to know Dave Boyle (Tim Robbins), who obviously cherishes family, friendship, and community and only has the best of intentions. Still, childhood trauma has tainted Dave with a darker side, which leads to his tragic actions. Complex characters will also be portrayed throughout a story with several different levels of emotion.

Another facet of hero development is defining what's at stake for her. **Stakes** are what the hero risks if she doesn't emerge triumphantly from the central conflict. By knowing what the stakes are, we often get a sense of what is most important to the hero. We also connect with her, given she will probably cling to the same human needs that we all do. Upon entering the second act, the hero might be risking life, love, knowledge, self-esteem, health, or personal fulfillment. Many stories will put multiple stakes on the table for the hero, and a good story will continue to **raise the stakes**, especially throughout the second act. In other words, the hero might begin Act II only aware that she is risking her job, but by the midpoint, perhaps, she learns that her life, too, is at stake. At the midpoint of *The Incredibles*, Mr. Incredible learns that Syndrome intends to launch an attack on his city with a lethal robot, and we learn that his own family—en route to rescue him—is now in serious jeopardy. Mind you, not only do stakes paint a human picture of the hero, but they also draw us further into the plot as we wonder in suspense if this person will succeed or experience devastating failure.

In most cases, **likeability** is considered to be a prerequisite for a hero. Heroes will be likeable or sympathetic to you because they are accessible; they portray the same human needs, desires, and fears that you have and they operate (or try to operate) within the boundaries of certain values that you and others in your community hold in esteem. In your reading, however, you will come across the occasional **antihero**, who may act outside the guidelines of your own moral or ethical status quo. Well-written antiheroes work, despite the likeability factor, because they still manifest wants and needs, a character arc, dimension, and their own sense of stakes. Antiheroes sometimes fascinate audiences (and readers) because they guide us through an alternate mindset in which uninhibited freedom, rebellion, vigilantism, or even anarchy reign supreme. In this modern life, we all live within the confines of rules, restrictions, guidelines, caveats, boundaries, and varying levels of oppression and repression. At once, the effective antihero provides us with both a degree of discomfort as we view the world against the grain and a degree of titillating escapism as we realize that life can be otherwise. A few memorable antiheroes are Travis Bickle (*Taxi Driver*), Han Solo (*Star Wars*), Bonnie Parker and Clyde Barrow (*Bonnie and Clyde*), Djay (*Hustle & Flow*), and Jack Sparrow (the *Pirates of the Caribbean* trilogy).

An author might also help us get to know a hero by including a **reflective character**—that is, a supporting character who is mainly there to listen to our hero as she voices her conflict, options, and future intentions. What the reflective character says about our hero will often tell us a lot about her, and this character is often one who urges change in the protagonist, thus contributing to her arc. The reflective character device is frequently utilized in classic "boy meets girl" romances and romantic comedies. Both boy and girl will have a sounding board or two to whom they can express their joy and anguish. To explore another Nora Ephron film, *Sleepless in Seattle* introduces us to Sam (Tom Hanks) and Annie (Meg Ryan), who voice the progress of their relationship to friends Jay (Rob Reiner) and Becky (Rosie

O'Donnell), respectively. Such supporting characters will often play the lead in their own subplots, and, in good material, will undergo a "mini-character arc," if you will.

The Villain

While all of the above contributes to the quality of the protagonist, it is often said that a hero is really only as good as the script's villain or **antagonist**. This character must represent the negation of everything the hero wants, needs, or stands for. He is the hero's absolute worst nightmare. A formidable opposite, he determines the stakes and will make or break the appeal of a script's plot.

Before going any further, be reminded that not all antagonists are people or characters. Look at any "creature feature," such as *Alien* or *Predator* (or *Alien vs. Predator*, for that matter), or any disaster movie such as *Volcano* or *The Day After Tomorrow*. The antagonists in *Apollo 13* are the physical and mechanical universe, while the heroes in *A Perfect Storm* go head to head with Mother Nature. In *Lorenzo's Oil*, it is a rare disease in their child that two parents must battle. Or examine *The Mosquito Coast*, in which Allie's (Harrison Ford) main foe is an internal demon: his own obsession. Within most of these films, there are certainly characters with shades of villainy or inner demons, but their involvement amounts to subplot and serves to add setbacks, reversals, and theme to the piece, whereas the antagonist is the main force behind the central conflict.

If, however, the antagonist is a person (or an anthropomorphized creature, in the case of some animation, an object), a good script will keep in mind that villains are people, too, and that this individual has been forced on his own "anti-journey" of sorts. While the hero's plot is formed by a series of actions and reactions to conflict wrought mainly by the antagonist, the villain's story represents a string of opposing actions and reactions. While the hero will be motivated by beliefs, tastes, hopes, fears, and so on, the antagonist will also be propelled by his own set of these characteristics. No interesting villain will commit evil simply because he *is* evil (not even "Dr. Evil" in the *Austin Powers* series). He will have his own agenda based on his own very human needs, and it is the hero who stands in the way of him achieving them. This rule applies to even the most comic-book of villains. Consider Magneto in the *X-Men* movies, who, based on experiences in World War II, is fearful for the survival of his own kind—the heavily ostracized Mutant population. His game plan— to annihilate humanity before humanity gets him—may not be the most moral, but one can see that he is driven by *concrete* needs and fears.

Like the hero, the antagonist will likely have his own reflective character with whom to share reactions and intentions. Often, we'll see a villain adorned with henchmen, sidekicks, yes-men, soldiers, and the like, who will not only serve as obstacles for our hero, but also paint an aura of extreme power, mystique, and loathing around the antagonist. Writers often make the mistake of including details about too many of these characters such that a reader will lose sense of who is whom. They all might begin to talk, act, and look alike to the extent that they lose their effect. A good script will collapse the antagonist's support team into a few distinct voices for a more effective punch and leave other followers in the background as a single but formidable force—almost a single character in itself.

Archetypes

In addition to the key protagonist and antagonist, there exists a spectrum of character patterns or functions that serve to help or hinder them throughout their conflict. While evaluating a screenplay, it is important to have a general sense of these basic **archetypes** in order to better decipher a character's relevance to a story (or irrelevance in some cases). Let's use examples from *The Lord of the Rings* trilogy as we define some of the archetypes.

Note that archetypes are fluid. A character may take the form of one or more of the following archetypes at one point in the story, only to appear as another later. (For more about these archetypes and others, read *The Writer's Journey*, by Christopher Vogler [Michael Wiese Productions], who does an exceptional job of detailing these character patterns and providing examples.)

In addition to the hero archetype, stories will include a **shadow figure**, or the hero's opposite. This shadow archetype can represent what the hero is in danger of becoming if he doesn't accomplish his goals (Gollum) and usually takes the form of antagonist but might also appear as one of the villain's lieutenants (Saruman), or even a friend of the hero (Boromir). Another archetype is that of the **mentor**, who will provide knowledge, nourishment, supplies, and anything else to aid a hero on his journey. Often a mentor will take the form of or contribute to the inciting incident, in which that character will supply initial encouragement regarding the conflict that is about to take place (Bilbo, Gandalf, Galadriel). In your reading, you will inevitably come across a mischievous **trickster** figure, essentially a prankster or rebel. Working against the status quo of the story's universe, the trickster will often deliver laughs to the story and, in his innate need to see things differently, make life difficult for our hero, either intentionally or inadvertently (Merry, Pippin, Gollum).

A trickster or shadow may also take the form of a **gatekeeper**. This type will serve as an obstacle or complication on the hero's path to the climactic showdown with his antagonist (Orcs, Ringwraiths, Shelob the spider). Without using wit, knowledge, and/or strength, the hero's journey could be abruptly ended by this inimical force. The way in which a hero reacts to a certain gatekeeper may be used to develop that character's virtues, flaws, tastes, and even his backstory. A shadow figure, trickster, mentor, or gatekeeper may also take the form of a **shapeshifter**. As the name suggests, a shapeshifter is one that changes its appearance along the way. One who might begin the story as a friend to our hero might gradually or suddenly become an enemy, or vice versa (again, Boromir, Gollum). Finally, mentor, trickster, shadow figure, and shapeshifter alike might also assume the form of the hero's **allies**. Naturally, allies cover the broad body of characters who stand by the hero's side as he faces his fears and foes (the entire Fellowship of the Ring).

Cardboard and Stereotyping

As a critical reader, note that it's you should expect to see some dimension in not only a hero or a villain. Whether a shadow, trickster, gatekeeper, ally, mentor, reflective, or otherwise, good characters will exhibit humanizing elements that make them seem real. In the real world, we all have specific characteristics that separate us from one another—in the way we talk, think, hope, fear, or pass time, down to more physical aspects. In the fictional world, so too will every well-written character be separated by these considerations. Those characters that do not "come off the page" in such a way are often called **flat** or **cardboard**. Flat characters will seem one note; they will have been written for a single, unsatisfying agenda: only to make us laugh, to stand in the way, to offer a clue, etc.

Often, a cardboard character is also a **stereotype**. I cannot tell you how many mob-related scripts I have read that include the likes of henchmen Luigi, Dominic, and Tony, who roam the story as ball-scratching, pasta-eating goons who love to whack people. Such material transparently strives to imitate successes such as *Goodfellas* or *The Sopranos*. However, writers often do not realize that those successes work because a refreshingly distinct human face has been put on each of its characters, most of whom don't exist as black and white/good and evil but somewhere in the more realistic gray zone. Other examples of stereotypes that I constantly come across are the good-looking frat boy or sorority chick, the gangsta rapper, the loner serial killer who was abused as a child, the troubled president of the United States, the corrupt Southern sheriff, the homosexual best friend. Certainly, there is nothing wrong with these types existing within a script, but without a new spin on their personality or description, they are doomed for evaluation as stereotypes.

The Ensemble

We have mostly been talking about the hero as a single person, but many scripts have been written to include multiple heroes, which could be called an **ensemble**. This is a cast of characters who embark on a separate or coinciding journey to create a whole story. Throughout an ensemble piece, one hero may become part of another hero's subplot or might even serve as another's antagonist or gatekeeper. A good ensemble piece will make sure that each hero's storyline intersects with the other's. Otherwise, a work could seem frustratingly scattered, and each hero's separate narrative could diminish the effect of the other's. Each hero should also complete a separate, clear arc.

For some great examples of ensemble work, watch Robert Altman's films, such as *Short Cuts* or *Gosford Park*. Other ensembles appear in *American Pie, Love Actually, Crash*, and Paul Thomas Anderson's *Boogie Nights* and *Magnolia*.

Character-Driven Scripts

If you were to quickly sum up the film *First Blood*, you would probably do so along the lines of this: "A wandering Vietnam vet is unjustly harassed by a small-town sheriff and forced to flee to the woods, where he fends off local law enforcement and an old mentor." Here, you would be describing the story in terms of its plot, because such a description would best encapsulate it. Most tales within the action, adventure, fantasy, horror, comedy, or romantic comedy genres could be described by a sketch of their plot. Thus, we would call this material **plot-driven**.

However, what if it's a story such as *The Big Chill*, in which not much really *happens*? One could say that this ensemble piece is about a few thirty-something college friends spending a weekend together after the death of a close friend and how the experience gently transforms each of them. Here, the emphasis is not on the plot, because there *isn't* much plot. Rather, this film is a story about people, their relationships to one another, and their respective inner journeys. Such stories are often categorized as **character-driven**, in which characters, especially their arcs, are the centerpieces.

In a character-driven work, you won't receive much distraction from action sequences, special effects, globe-trotting locations, lavish set pieces, or broad slapstick. That's not to say that a character study won't include one or more of those elements. (Consider *Solaris* and its futuristic setting, mostly in space.) But the spotlight isn't so much on superficial goals (e.g., getting the girl, walking away with the case of cash, solving the mystery) as it is on the intimate, internal transformation of the protagonist(s). There are countless other examples, but some produced character-driven films that come to mind are: *Midnight Cowboy, Harold & Maude, The Ice Storm, The Apostle, The Hours, Lost in Translation, Napoleon Dynamite*, and *The Devil Wears Prada*.

Finding Nemo: *A Case Study of Structure in Relation to Character*

Having addressed both structure and character, now is a good time to dissect one very well-known film, specifically exploring its use of the three-act template and how character work is folded into it.

Act I

Everyday world: After the trauma of having lost his wife and all but one of his progeny, we find Marlin living in fear of the open ocean, of taking chances, and of trusting anyone but himself—all to the extent that he has become an overbearing figure to his son, Nemo.

Inciting incident: Nemo goes to school and is tempted by the freedom it could bring him.

Turning point 1: Nemo is captured by a mysterious human diver. Fueled by emotion and trauma, Marlin goes after him.

Act II

IIA: Marlin hooks up with Dory and goes off in search of Nemo, braving many elements in dangerous open water—a worst nightmare come true for Marlin. After surviving an encounter with both a hungry shark and a lethal bottom-dweller, Marlin and Dory are finally able to lift enough information from the diver's mask to point them in Nemo's direction. Meanwhile, Nemo attempts to survive and prove himself among the others in his new habitat, the aquarium. After successfully swimming over the mountain of fire, he is finally accepted and given the task of stopping the filter system.

Midpoint: Dory has been a big help, but Marlin remains as blind as ever to her contribution to his cause. Floundering in his own fear and mistrust, he directs them into a minefield of deadly jellyfish rather than following someone else's intuition. By returning to the fray to rescue Dory, Marlin shows that he may actually care and that he possesses the potential for bravery. He is halfway through his arc. But both are severely wounded, if not killed. Back in the fish tank, Nemo fails his sabotage mission and nearly dies in the process. Gill, a buddy also from the ocean, declares their struggle over.

IIB: Marlin awakens with the help of a sea turtle. He thinks Dory is on her death bed but is delighted to find that she has recovered and is just playing hide and seek with a bunch of hatchlings. Marlin can't help but edge a little closer to trusting Dory and fearing a little less. A big leap in their quest, they're now on the EAC (East Australian Current), heading straight for Nemo, though directly into the danger zone, as well. When they finally jump off the current, it's apparently a straight shot to Nemo, but details about their own location suddenly become murky and they are swallowed by a whale, leaving Marlin to pass another major test. Nemo gets word that his father is on his way and begins to see the man in a new light. Invigorated by Marlin's efforts, Nemo braves the filter again and succeeds, but all hope is lost when their keeper places a new, impenetrable filtration system in the tank.

Turning point 2: In the belly of the whale, Marlin again lives in fear of taking a chance with Dory. Still, for the first time in a long while, he fully lets go—literally, of the whale's tongue, and figuratively, of much of his fear. Hence, he is rewarded and finds himself deposited into the waters of Sydney via the whale's blowhole. But now he is into the "hornet's nest" of his innermost fears. Meanwhile, Nemo picks up a little trick for resisting a human net, but it's not enough, as he's scooped into a plastic bag in time for the arrival of the nasty little girl, Darla.

Act III

With the help of a new friend, Nigel the pelican, Marlin and Dory try to make their way to Nemo at the dentist's office. They arrive inside the office and the bird almost manages to scoop up Nemo, but it just misses. Nemo survives Darla but ends up going down the drain along with Marlin's hope of ever reuniting with his son. The father is so defeated that he again reverts back to his old mentality by rejecting Dory. But Dory connects with Nemo after the little one is shot out of the drainage pipe, manages to remember the kid's name, and delivers him to his father.

Climax: Though reunited, father and son are once again forced to brave the human wrath as Dory is caught in a trawling net. Marlin lets go of Nemo so the boy can go help Dory, accepting that his son can accomplish things on his own. Drawing on a lesson recently learned, Nemo inspires the entire trapped school of fish to swim against their captors, resulting in everyone's escape.

Resolution: We find Marlin and Nemo happily back in their old neighborhood, Marlin with new self-esteem and encouraging his son to seek adventure, and Nemo with a new appreciation for his father. Dory has moved into the neighborhood, too, and has earned a new level of acceptance.

Finding Nemo
(2003, Buena Vista Pictures, Buena Vista Home Entertainment)
Original Story by Andrew Stanton
Screenplay by Andrew Stanton, Bob Peterson, David Reynolds
Co-directed by Lee Unkrich
Directed by Andrew Stanton

By reviewing *Finding Nemo*, one can begin to see how well-written character, structure, and plot interrelate to contribute to a greater whole. With an awareness of those three crucial pieces, you are well on your way to grasping the entire picture.

4

The Supporting Elements

We have reviewed the three biggest pieces an analyst should keep in mind while critiquing the complex puzzle of a screenplay, but there is an array of smaller pieces that, in good material, should adequately supplement them. These supporting elements both influence and are dependent upon the success of the other three. The following is a rundown of these crucial items.

Pace

Pace is the tempo or rhythm of a story. While reading a script, if the story holds your attention without your mind wandering to the refrigerator, bathroom, or last night's date, then it's probably well-paced. But, as a critical reader, you should be able to voice what it is about the pace that's keeping you on your heinie. Naturally, a fast pace fosters a feeling of high adrenaline, urgency, suspense, or progress; a slow pace suggests contemplation, information, reflection, despair, or stagnation. Pace is affected by both structure and the arrangement of scenes from one to the next within the plot. Quite often, a poorly structured script will also feel poorly paced due to a lack of the guided ebb and flow of conflict and character that tight structure nurtures. Too much fast or slow pacing within a long block of scenes could also turn you off as a reader. Too fast will tend to deprive you of a sense of emotion and thought and could lead to confusion, while too slow detracts from that sense of forward energy.

Given the contemporary MTV appetites of mass audiences and executives alike (call them what you will), an overall quick pace is the preferred mode, and authors will often do their best to cater to that. A writer might use a sequence or sequences to pick up the pace. While this device might temporarily pick up the tempo, it doesn't always help the overall pace of a script. While reading, watch out for the chase sequence or athletic montage that's in there for its own sake without really contributing to the forward progression of the story. A script that lacks conflict from scene to scene will certainly flounder in slow pace. I have read scripts in which good things happen to the heroes for pages or in which characters simply converse without any friction. Needless to say, in these cases, the material drags.

A script will also suffer from poor pacing if it doesn't provide **urgency**. Urgency emerges when a protagonist has X amount of time to do Y before Z happens. (Hence, urgency and stakes [i.e., the Z] often go hand-in-hand when evaluating a script.) Urgency within individual scenes or sequences certainly helps to move things along and can generate comedy and/or suspense at a certain point in the story. Can the thief rob the safe before the homeowner returns? Can the woman make it to the train before the love of her life leaves town forever? But an overall, well-paced script will be propelled by a sense of urgency that spans an entire act or an entire narrative throughline. For some simple examples, at the beginning of Act II, we might learn that our hero has three months to find the cure to his rare illness or risk death, or that our hero has to discover the identity of a killer before more people are murdered. A good screenplay will then ratchet up the urgency as the plot progresses, perhaps by bringing the stakes even closer to home as the hero gets closer to his goal (e.g., the ill hero suddenly develops a debilitating complication or the killer murders our hero's best friend).

Quite often, an author will bring urgency to a new high during Act III by introducing a new **ticking clock**. This urgency device might literally be a clock. See every James Bond film, for example. Can Bond do battle with the villain, save the girl, and escape the fortress before a time bomb destroys the world? An effective ticking clock, however, needn't be so blatant. In *The Graduate*, Elaine's marriage ceremony provides the ticking clock for Ben. As the wedding moves along, can Ben get there before she's lost forever?

Dialogue

Dialogue is simply the language every character uses to converse with the others. The way in which characters speak can truly make or break a script-reading experience. It might serve as a screenplay's Achilles heel or its saving grace. I have recommended writers and dismissed others based solely on the quality of their dialogue. I have witnessed studio executives proclaiming, "The story's okay, but her dialogue is beautiful! Let's get this writer in here!" When reading, the best way to evaluate dialogue is by asking yourself three simple questions: 1) Is it natural? 2) Is it distinct from character to character? 3) Is it necessary?

In real life, people usually don't talk in long sentences without interruption. Even when telling a story or expressing feelings, chances are, someone else will chime in with their own two cents, even if it's just a "yeah" or an "mmhm" or an "of course." Unfortunately, you will come across many writers who have lost touch with (or never learned) the fact that most people talk "rapid fire," if you will, spitting out a word here, half a sentence there, before someone else interpolates or overlaps. Extended monologues rarely happen in natural speak, nor is it common for a person to flit about talking to himself for long periods. These unnatural devices are best left to the melodrama of stage plays and soap operas.

Sometimes, the only thing that seems to separate one character from another are their names. (Remember those stereotyped mobsters I was telling you about in the previous chapter?) In which case, you as a reader will inevitably feel lost in the who's who of the script's cast. Some readers get so perplexed that they're forced to take notes, even make charts, as they go along in order to keep track of the characters—not a good sign for the writer. Well-crafted dialogue will foster **character distinction**. No two people talk exactly alike. We all have our personal speech preferences, ticks, tones, and drives that separate us from each other, as should every character in a script. In *The Squid and the Whale*, for example, William Baldwin's "Ivan" finishes many of his sentences by calling people "Brother." Upon looking at Ivan's dialogue in the screenplay, you might immediately recognize him by this quirk. If you can tell who's talking based not on their name but on their speech, then the dialogue is working to a degree.

On the other hand, you will find many writers who rely on dialogue as a crutch, forgetting that *the medium for which they are writing is, above all, a visual one.* (*Do not forget this golden rule while reading a script.*) Dialogue can often feel **expository** or **heavy-handed** as a writer stretches a character's lines to reveal plot, backstory, or inner feelings. While critiquing a script, ask yourself if these ideas—a certain emotion, memory, or event—could have been told by *showing* them rather than the characters saying them. This is one of the reasons why earlier I praised the example in *Ice Age*: no dialogue is exchanged, yet through stylized visuals we learn so much about Manfred's backstory and motivation. Many authors will also toil with redundant dialogue. The writer might have taken the time to show/describe a certain event in the text but goes on to have a character describe what we can easily see. A good script will utilize the power of visualizing a character's subtle expression, action, or reaction to tell us what needs to be said.

Believability

If I told you that human reality is nothing but an illusion created by machines that have enslaved us, you would never believe it. But *The Matrix* manages to **suspend disbelief** by fleshing out a new world early in the story—its rules, do's, don'ts, cans, and cannots—and then stays true to those powers and limitations throughout the rest of the story. (Okay, the two follow-up films are a whole other story, but the first *Matrix*, at least, gets the job done.)

In the world of storytelling, writers will often push the boundaries of imagination to touch on some very down-to-earth, universal concepts and emotions. The question is, then, how does the author keep us believing along the way? Whether it's a very human story in the present day or an extravagant sci-fi romp, a good script will convince you that the events unfolding on the pages are possible. To do so, the writer will have to establish the rules of her world within the first forty or so pages. If magical things are going to transpire, then a well-written script will, at the very least, hint to us in the first act that magic exists within the story's universe. Otherwise, a magical element suddenly introduced around the midpoint or later might taint a script's believability. Or, if a character is introduced as possessing certain skills but doesn't even consider using them when he really needs them, then it would become an unbelievable situation.

I have read many scripts that take place within our reality and tell stories in which someone commits what is obviously a crime (assault, robbery). Based on the realistic, present-day universe painted by the author, all logic will tell me that this character would never get away with it without some sort of retribution or legal fallout, yet he walks away un-approached by the law, hence rendering the material unbelievable.

Predictability

In 98 percent of all scripts you read, you will probably be able to predict the outcome: the hero gets the girl, defeats the villain, survives the disaster, wins the match, or what have you. What makes a script truly predictable or unpredictable, however, is how the plot gets you to that outcome. An unpredictable script will throw reversals, curve balls, twists, pitfalls, and seemingly insurmountable "near-death" experiences at you, leaving you to wonder: Now how are they going to get around this one? Likewise, an unpredictable script's characters will sidestep or conquer obstacles in innovative ways, leaving you to remark: Wow, I couldn't have seen that one coming. A predictable script, on the other hand, will establish a route to a desired outcome and then follow that path without deviation, or it will "borrow" from classic predecessors without introducing anything new to the genre. You might, for example, come across a Western that, half way through, has foreshadowed that all events are leading to a climactic duel along the dusty main street. We've seen this before. If that duel doesn't do anything but show a few characters shooting it out and a hero emerging victorious, then what you have is an extreme case of predictability.

Payoff

A tight script will make sure that a reader is rewarded with **payoff**. Payoff is a logical, satisfying wrap-up to information that is planted earlier in the story. This information can take the form of a visual, dialogue, or even a character. There are few, if any, genres that don't rely on setup and payoff in their plot, but the device is especially relied on for laughs in comedy, both physical and dialogue-based. For example, in *Something's Gotta Give*, Dr. Mercer (Keanu Reeves) tells horny Harry (Jack Nicholson) that, as a rule of thumb, heart attack patients such as him shouldn't have sex until they can climb a full set of stairs. Nicholson's subsequent drained expression at the foot of a daunting beach stairway provides some chuckles at the character's expense, not to mention a measure of his rehabilitation in further attempts.

In mysteries, thrillers, and dramas, information is often introduced to lead us in one direction, only to pay off in a completely unexpected way, rendering a twist. (For those of you haven't seen *Mystic River* and still intend to one of these days: *spoiler alert*.) In the film, cops Sean (Kevin Bacon) and Whitey (Laurence Fishburn) learn that Brendan Harris' now deceased father had a gun—the same gun responsible for killing Brendan's girlfriend, Katie Markham. All logic suggests that Brendan is the one who killed Katie, but when Brendan goes to look for it, we're just as shocked as he is to discover that the gun is not there. While the gun information corrals our attention toward Brendan, we realize only when he does that his quiet brother also had access to the weapon and used it. The fact that brother Silent Ray is the killer creates a powerful twist.

Silent Ray's setup as a character pays off to aid the twist, too. We are introduced to this mute, seemingly harmless kid who is content to mind his own business. We only see him a few times and, early in the story, probably regard him as one who is mixed in for texture—in Brendan's life and in the community. Still, if that's all he was, then he might come across as excess fat in a story already infused with so many figures. But the author knew what he was doing when he planted this unobtrusive character into the fabric of his narrative.

Regardless of the genre, the payoff device keeps a story contained. To sample *Training Day* again, early in the story we watch Jake interrupt his ride with his new mentor in order to rescue a young woman being raped in an alleyway. In itself, the event might serve to develop Ethan Hawke's character as the idealist rookie that he is (and conversely, Denzel Washington's character as detached and hardened). Yet, it could have been perceived as a random sidestep in the storyline were it not for the fortuitous discovery much later that the girl he saved happens to be the cousin of the very man who is about to execute him. In the intense bathtub scene, Jake's would-be assassin finds the girl's wallet, which the rookie pocketed at the scene of the crime. Now, imagine the man with the gun coming across the wallet without any setup—without the alley scene. The occurrence would come across as overly convenient with no backstory to it. In sum, information setup that is not paid off could weigh down the material with loose ends. Information that is paid off but not set up correctly could make for a plot hole, plot contrivance, or confusion about a character.

Tone

A script's **tone** is its overall feel or mood. Some words you might use to describe tone include: somber, dark, moody, gloomy, or harsh; upbeat, warm, light, optimistic, spiritual, or quirky. If I were describing tone in *The Sixth Sense*, I would call it hushed, intimate, and tense. I might label *Chicago* as naughty and *Like Water for Chocolate* or *Big Fish* as magical.

Whatever feel you derive from a piece, a deft storyteller will maintain that undercurrent from first page to last. If not, the material is probably guilty of **tone shift**. If something starts out as a wacky comedy only to become gravely serious in the latter half, that would be tone shift. Many dramas are in danger of beginning edgy only to melt into sappiness. Critics either praised or pounced on *Adaptation*, which spends its first two acts as a quirky comedy but dramatically shifts into a wacky buddies-on-the-run flick. Look at *The Apartment*, which begins as a light comedy, but dips into serious dramatic territory after Shirley MacLaine tries to kill herself and Jack Lemmon struggles to revive her. After that, the comedy reverts back to its old self to complete the film. ·

These are instances of tone shift that have, for the most part, been accepted by audiences and critics. In most cases, however, tone shift is regarded by script readers as unappealing or unsettling in that it sells us one way, sucking us into a mood and mindset, only to deliver us a different product later.

Point of View

We all know the classic points of view in literature. There's *first person*, in which the author assumes the mind of one character and speaks with "I"; *third person, omniscient*, in which an author, speaking with "he" and "she", accesses the inner thoughts and backgrounds of all characters and may add comment on events and people in the story; *third person, limited*, which is similar to the omniscient perspective, but the narrator only reveals internal information about one or a select few characters; and *third person, detached*, which offers simple, objective reporting on actions in the story.

In the film world, for which scripts are written, there will always be an audience watching from the fourth wall—all of whom will be thinking in terms of "he" and "she." It would be nearly impossible to create a story for the screen in the first person. To date, the film that has come the closest is *Lady in the Lake*, a 1947 adaptation of a Raymond Chandler novel in which the camera assumes the point of view of its protagonist, Philip Marlowe, at all times. In other words, we never see Marlowe because we're supposed to be Marlowe. For the most part, however, movies are written in various shades resembling the literary third person. Depending on the desired effect, we might be somewhat privy to the minds and activities of many or most in the cast. In such cases, we know the intentions and general movement of the protagonist and his allies as well as those of the antagonist and his support, rendering an almost omniscient perspective. It's probably the most widely used point of view in everything from broad action flicks to small ensemble pieces.

There are other scripts that follow a single character or two from scene to scene, making such material closer to the "third person, limited" point of view. Character-driven scripts will often utilize this perspective. Except for perhaps two or three quick moments, *The Station Agent* features its main character in every scene. Mysteries or thrillers, such as *Seven* or *Memento*, may also employ a limited point of view, in which we pick up information and experience surprise right along with the main character(s).

A detached point of view isn't all that common, though mockumentaries such as *Waiting for Guffman* have been known to use it. Such stories are told under the guise of objective reporting but actually make a statement while winking at the audience.

As with tone, so too can point of view experience a shift—from many characters to one, one to many, or from character to character. Some films do it deliberately and get away with it. The classic example is *Psycho*, in which we begin the story with Janet Leigh, believing her to be our heroine. But the film jostles us when her character (Marion) is killed, leaving old Norman Bates to pick up the reins for the rest of the story. The effect is unsettling. More recently, *The Village* shows a flux in perspective by obliterating Joaquin Phoenix's role in the film after he is stabbed at the midpoint and tossing the baton to Bryce Dallas Howard.

Still, point-of-view shift is an unorthodox method that is more likely to disorient or interrupt the flow of a story and is usually generated by more inexperienced writers. Imagine watching a film that begins with one character's voice-over—indicating that this is probably his story or that events will unfold through his eyes—but somebody else becomes the source of voice-over in the middle. Consciously or subconsciously, you would probably find yourself stewing in discomfort for lack of a solid anchor or foundation from which to read the work.

Theme

At the core of every story, you will hopefully discover the author's voice and what she wants to say with this script or its **theme**. If a script tells us nothing about the "human experience," then you will probably close its pages feeling empty and untouched.

Themes you will commonly encounter in screenplays include humanity's ability to overcome immense adversity (i.e., those films commonly marketed as "a story about the triumph of the human spirit"), you can't judge a book by its cover, love conquers all, be yourself, follow your destiny, live life to the fullest, man is cruel to man, respect nature, know your limitations, and everyone has self-worth.

Statement of theme is more likely to emerge from character arc and via interaction in the subplot than from the center ring of the plot, as subplot allows for characters to make a pit stop and stand back to reflect on the central conflict. Theme should gently waft out of a script rather than hit us between the eyes. Few people watch a movie to be preached to. If an author repeats the message on numerous occasions, then we are probably hearing a little too much of that writer's voice. A good script will leave us to deduce the author's intent without her actually saying it through a character.

The way in which a writer uses her characters could draw out unintended and often unsavory themes. I have read countless scripts in which all the good guys are white males and the bad guys are . . . well, girls . . . or Hispanic, African-American, or Asian. What those stories might say to an impressionable moviegoer is that white males do and should dominate—a destructive message by most standards. The TV show *24* got into trouble when it portrayed a family of Muslims as a terrorist sleeper cell. Had there been a Muslim agent or some other Muslim working for the "good guys," then perhaps the story choice might not have endured so much condemnation by Muslim groups, but there was no balancing figure, and so the message could have been perceived as: all Muslims are terrorists.

Upon reading some scripts that fall into this category, I never thought the writers were intentionally bad or racist people. They were often just tapping into unfortunate stereotypes. A good writer will know to balance her cast with more diverse choices. If you come across a minority villain, therefore, look for a balancing character on the protagonist's side, and vice versa.

As an offshoot of theme, **motif** might also appear in a script. A motif is an image or concept that is repeated throughout a story. Motifs don't typically come with a message, but they can be layered with symbolism or emotion. They can provide a window to a screenwriter's artistic intentions and can be used to enhance suspense, drama, and comedy or add texture to tone, setting, and visuals. Study Martin Scorsese's *The Aviator*, for example, for that film's rich use of motif, including hands, crashes, and film imagery projected onto Howard Hughes' face and body. What these motifs do or mean to you as a viewer is up to you, while Mr. Scorsese had his own reasons for including them in the story. Many sci-fi pictures subscribe to the concept of humanity versus machines as a recurring motif.

Formatting

I have had to read scripts written by hand, formatted like a play, stained with coffee, and bound like a fourth-grade science project. It's all fun and games until someone has to read it. When you get a three-ring binder adorned with all sorts of flashy artwork and marketing suggestions (e.g., a superhero drawn on the front), then you know you're in for a painful read. Okay, in this case, odds are you can judge a book by its cover.

There is no absolute, but a standard hard-copied screenplay should come to you on white, three-hole-punch paper, bound by two or three brass fasteners. The script might be covered by plain card stock, but that's about it as far as binding goes. (The exception to these specifications might be given to the Brits, bless them, who, for decades, have somehow been getting away with legal-size paper and brilliant metal screw fasteners that you can only seem to purchase in Europe.)

Whether in hard copy or electronic form, standard formatting inside the pages includes black, 12-point Courier font and margins of approximately one inch in any direction. Text or narrative (i.e., visuals and action) is written the full width within the side margins. Character names are capitalized and centered directly above dialogue, which has cropped margins (approximately 3.5 inches from the left, 2.5 inches from the right) to occupy only the middle of the page.

Other details to look for include: Voiceover (V.O.), implying narration that other characters can't hear; Off Screen (O.S.), implying sound or dialogue whose source we can't see but that all characters in the visual space can hear; MORE, found at the bottom of a page that ends with dialogue to suggest there is more to come on the next page (optional); CONTINUED, found at the top of the page to indicate a continuation of dialogue from the bottom of the previous (also optional); (beat), which suggests a moment for pause, emotion, or reaction. Scene headings precede a new scene and/or location and include: INT. (interior) or EXT. (exterior)–SETTING–TIME OF DAY, all in caps.

In some scripts, you might find suggested camera angles in the text such as C.U. (close up), ANGLE ON, or PULL BACK (i.e., dolly backwards), as well as editing suggestions such as CUT TO or DISSOLVE TO. Other than FADE IN and FADE OUT, these details are generally discouraged nowadays. Directors and editors are increasingly territorial over the choice of camera angle and splice. Likewise, screenwriters are urged not to include specific names of songs, since one never knows if a company will be able to secure the rights to such a tune (the exception being if a particular song or song title is absolutely integral to the telling of the story and/or the development of a certain character). These drawbacks won't necessarily make or break the quality of a story, but it's worth a sentence of mention if you're offering a complete critique.

Other no-no's include overuse of parentheses to indicate emotion or action within lines of dialogue, bold or italicized font, and of course, typos. Fortunately, screenwriting software such as Final Draft or Movie Magic has significantly minimized substandard formatting. (See Appendix C for resources where you can find completed scripts in proper format.)

Most important, you will know a writer has potential if the script is simply a good read. Long paragraphs of detailed text can be taxing to a reader. Good text will have literary merit in itself while it influences pace and tone and guides a reader's imagination through individual actions and visuals, much the same way a director will steer a viewer's eyes and ears.

Concept and Marketability

If a story concept is fresh and could be sold to millions at the megaplex with the face of a big-name star leading the way, then this element might carry about as much weight as the success of all the others put together. Indeed, on many occasions, I have covered a script that is poorly executed in a number of ways but still believed the material to be **marketable** based on its core idea and castable roles. "Marketable" basically means that a film can be easily sold to a large, identifiable **target audience**, increasing its chances that the film will succeed in the box office and video store.

Marketable concepts are those that are considered to have universal appeal. They usually revolve around one or more of these classic formulas: boy meets girl, boy gets girl (*The Wedding Singer*); David versus Goliath (*Erin Brockovich; Die Hard*); Man versus Nature (*Jaws; The Day After Tomorrow*); Stranger in a Strange Land (*The Last Samurai; The Chronicles of Narnia: The Lion, The Witch, and The Wardrobe*); opposites attract (*Something's Gotta Give*); opposites thrown together/buddy-buddy (*Midnight Run; Bad Boys; Grumpy Old Men*); revenge (*Double Jeopardy; Man on Fire*); the quest or Odyssey (*Apocalypse Now; Finding Nemo; Lord of the Rings* trilogy); Pandora's Box (*Jumanji; Click*); the secret (*The Truth About Cats and Dogs; Tootsie*); sudden powers for the unlikely soul (*Spiderman; Bruce Almighty*); coming of age (*Stand By Me; Bend It Like Beckham; American Pie*).

Scripts that cling to the rules of three-act structure, borrow from predecessors of its genre, and seem to have been plugged into one of the above-mentioned scenarios are sometimes referred to as **formulaic**. Readers and critics alike often pan formulaic stories, because they can be unoriginal and predictable. But at the same time, studios are usually hungry for such "recycled" material, because they do often generate a box-office draw. It is something that has been sold successfully before, and they know how to sell it again.

A formulaic script might also be labeled as **high concept**, meaning that the writer has created a story that can be summed up in a pat sentence and is of a widely popular genre (usually comedy, romantic comedy, or action). Take *Click*: A young, hardworking architect stumbles upon a remote control that enables him to fast forward through or rewind to certain moments in his life. Or *Die Hard*: A New York cop tries to rescue hostages from terrorists in a high rise. You read one of those sentences and you just know that many, many people could be sold on the concept. Like formulaic, high concept isn't necessarily negative or positive. It just depends on the client for whom you are reading. Studios gobble up high-concept material that can be neatly packaged and peddled to the masses. Hey, *Click* and *Die Hard* did well, right? But for every one of those successes, you will come across thousands of scripts that are equally high concept but deficient in many of the other facets of screenwriting listed in this section.

Target audiences are described by the use of demographic factors including age, gender, race, ethnicity, and geography. Many studio pics target that nebulous group called the **mainstream**, which is to say, everybody and their mother. A mainstream film will please—or at least try to please—a heaping cross section of the male and female population from young to old, coast to coast, border to border, white to black, to Asian to Latino. All in the name of the bottom line. Within the mainstream, teens to twenty-nine-year-olds (approximately), both male and female, are generally considered to be the most lucrative market (although in the television world, eighteen- to forty-nine-year-olds are the primary target). Males in this category are apt to flock to big-budget action, horror, thriller, and sci-fi flicks. Comic book– and video game–based concepts such as *Resident Evil, House of the Dead*, and *Hellboy* are marketed heavily toward this thrill-seeking group. Females in those age ranges will often accompany male friends and siblings to the above genres but are equally likely to rush to a theater to see romantic comedies, romantic dramas, or "chick flicks" such as *A Walk to Remember, Waiting to Exhale, John Tucker Must Die*, or *The Devil Wears Prada*.

But studios, small distributors, and independent producers can't and won't always target the general masses. There are too many stories out there that, if produced and marketed well, could make financial sense for an outfit. Hence, if they can't make it for Everyone, they will make it for Someone. Family or children's films will, by name, target preteens or younger and their parents, while dramas and some thrillers are usually aimed at folks in their late twenties and above. It is rare that you will find a feature film script that specifically targets baby boomers or older, as this demographic is considered less likely to shell out the money and energy at the Megaplex. Nevertheless, a few titles have focused on this niche, including: *The Bridges of Madison County, Memoirs of a Geisha*, and *Something's Gotta Give*. As for race or ethnicity, it's not often that you will come across a film written for a specific minority group, though exceptions such as *My Family* and *Selena* clearly focused on attracting Latino crowds and *Soul Food, Eve's Bayou*, and *Friday* were initially geared toward African-Americans.

Another niche group to keep in mind is what is often called the **art house** or **specialty film** demographic. This slice is usually a mature crowd (late twenties and up) who live in medium to large cities where one or more theaters cater to their appetite for foreign, low-budget, and/or independently produced fare. Character-driven material is often earmarked for this crowd.

In your reading, you might be handed a script that you feel is geared toward one niche but also demonstrates **crossover potential**, meaning that if someone gambles on it, word of its merits might spill into another target audience—hopefully the mainstream—and they'll tell their friends, who will tell their friends, who will tell their friends.... Some crossover sensations that come to mind are: *Cinema Paradiso; The Full Monty; Life Is Beautiful; Waking Ned Devine; Crouching Tiger, Hidden Dragon; My Big Fat Greek Wedding; Brokeback Mountain, and Little Miss Sunshine.*

With plot, structure, character, marketability, and their supporting elements under your belt, now would be a good time to grab a few produced screenplays (see Appendix C for some ideas how) and watch a few films while keeping each of these aspects closely in mind. The more you can practice critical thought, the better, as the next step is to pen your analysis within standard coverage format.

SECTION II
What's in Coverage?

THE NUTS AND BOLTS OF WRITING STORY ANALYSIS

There is no one set industry template for coverage, but you will find that the differences among clients' expectations are smaller than the similarities. Most coverage will include three main components:

1. The cover page

2. The synopsis

3. Comments

An additional, fourth component called the **character breakdown** may be requested by your client and will be discussed in the final chapter of this section.

Typically assembled in the above order, each of the three components serves a different purpose, requires a different angle of thought, and poses its own set of challenges.

5

The Top Sheet—
A Look Inside Your Coverage

What coverage is to the screenplay, a top sheet is to the coverage: a brief glance of what is inside. If someone doesn't like what she sees in the coverage, she may not read the screenplay. Likewise, if someone is turned off by what is described on your top sheet, she might not even dip into the analysis.

Of the three main coverage components, the top sheet (also called "cover page") is most likely to vary from client to client. Still, it is usually more the format of the cover page than the content itself that will differ. See Appendix A for some format possibilities.

The Top Third

To cover all bases, let's take care of the really easy part of the top sheet first. At the top of your cover page, you may be required to put a centered heading with the name of your employer's company and, under that, indicate that this report is indeed coverage or "Story Department Coverage." After that, you will be expected to include the following bits of information, usually arranged in two columns and with a space skipped in between each:

Title
Here is where you put the script's name, preferably in all caps. If the template given to you there has no line for "Based on" and the

material is an adaptation (from a novel, article, manuscript, short story or what have you), then insert your own "Based on TITLE, by Joe Shmoe" directly under the script title.

Story Analyst

Yes, this is you. It might also be listed on the cover sheet as "Analyst" or simply "Reader." Just put in your name. Although, funny enough, I have had a few story analysts work for me who would rather insert a nom de plume to maintain anonymity, because they are concerned that some writer or producer will find them, chew them out for their harsh critique of their work, and/or ruin their careers. Trust me—, I have *never* seen this happen in my fifteen years of experience in the industry and with thousands of scripts under my belt. But, it is an option for the paranoid set. Conversely, coverage services or agencies might *insist* that you use a different name, initials, or even an analyst number to keep outsiders from judging or stealing you. We will talk about that a little more in the third section of this book.

Form

This is where you indicate the form in which the writing arrived on your desk. Chances are, you will just type in "screenplay" or "sp," but you might also end up reading some of the following: teleplay (a screenplay intended for delivery as a TV movie that will usually include denoted Act breaks for the sake of advertisers); manuscript, book, or novel; magazine article; treatment; one-hour episodic (for TV); half-hour sitcom; comic book.

Draft

If a draft is indicated, it will appear on the cover page, either with a number (First, Second, etc.) or a date or both. Sometimes, an author might call it "First Draft, Revised" to suggest that the work has been polished but not completely rewritten. If you cannot find a draft or date on the cover page, just leave the space blank.

Pages

This is where you indicate the number of pages (excluding the covers). If there is no draft denoted, this figure could become more significant, as it may be the only indicator of which draft has been covered.

Period

Sometimes "Circa." This is the *When* of the story. Be as specific as you can without occupying more than a couple of lines within the column. If, for example, it is a story that takes place over the course of 1967–1972, just insert those years, or call it "Late 60s/Early 70s." If, as in *Bill and Ted's Excellent Adventure*, it jumps all over time, just offer each year covered, or even an era, such as Greek Empire, Napoleonic Era, The Civil War.

To indicate that a story takes place in the present is acceptable if it occurs within about five years. "The Future," "Sometime in the near future," and "Distant Future" work, too, though you should offer year(s) if provided. What you enter for period is a bit of a judgment call, but know that your client could be looking at this line closely, because the period of the proposed film could be a major factor in its budgeting and overall appeal.

Setting

Sometimes "Locale." This is the *Where* of the story. Again, be as specific as you can but keep it within a couple of lines. Do not get caught up in mentioning settings that only occupy a minute portion of the story. If it is about a road trip across seven states in the United States, but New York City and Los Angeles are featured prominently in the first and third acts, then you might say, "Los Angeles, New York City, highways and back roads of the United States."

Genre

Genre provides a means of categorizing a script based on its tone, concept, and content. The long list of standard genres includes: Comedy, Romantic Comedy, Drama, Horror, Action, Adventure, Fantasy, Family, Western, Mystery, Crime, Thriller, Animation, War, and Science Fiction. For a comprehensive list of examples of produced films within each of these categories, check out resources such as IMDb.com or the latest volume of *Video Hound's Golden Movie Retriever* where you can browse film titles by genre.

However, due to the endless quest for original material, many scripts will arrive on your lap in hybridized form. For example, an alternately serious and light script might be labeled as a Drama-Comedy or Dramedy. You might even go a step further and call a script a Romantic Dramedy if it focuses on a relationship (*The Graduate; The Family Stone*). Thriller might be preceded by any of its companion genres (e.g., Sci-fi/Thriller, Comedy/Thriller, Action/Thriller, Horror/Thriller). Action/Adventure is one I'm sure you've heard, as is Sci-fi/Horror (*Alien*). Naturally, some are less likely than others to be melded. Past *Love at First Bite* or *So I Married an Axe Murderer*, I'm not sure you are going to come across too many Romantic Comedy/Horror stories, though horror-comedies that spoof the genre (pioneered by *Young Frankenstein* and followed more recently by the *Scary Movie* franchise or *Shaun of the Dead*) are occasionally popular. Sci-fi/Westerns (*Wild, Wild West*) have been written, believe it or not, but they are far from common. Even Vampire/Westerns have appeared on the market, such as Sony Screen Gems' *Priest*.

There are other offshoots and subcategories that may help you further qualify genre. Stick "Period" in front of Drama or Comedy to indicate that it takes place somewhere between ten years ago and the dawn of time (*Gosford Park*). Place "Epic" in front of Drama, Adventure, or Fantasy to suggest a story of wide scope—one that spans a period of time, often with a cast of several and thousands of extras (*Lawrence of Arabia; Lord of the Rings*). Under Horror or Thriller, you might come across a Slasher, such as *Saw* or *Texas Chainsaw Massacre*, implying that some human (or near-human) is reaping a large body count among a group of young people. Other Thrillers might qualify as a Heist movie (*Inside Man, The Thomas Crown Affair*). Some stories you might call a Road Movie (e.g., *Rain Man, Forces of Nature, The Sure Thing*). Stories of this ilk have developed as a separate genre, though you might want to modify them with "Comedic" or "Dramatic." One other to keep in mind is the Biopic: usually a dramatic and somewhat true account of someone's life, such as *Ghandi, Walk the Line, Ray,* or *Dragon: The Bruce Lee Story*.

Unless you are simply *way* off, there is no right or wrong in the naming of genre. One person's Drama may be another's Comedy. One person's Horror may be another's Thriller. How many times have you gone to a video store or searched online for a certain Comedy only to find it listed with the Action movies? Like Period and Setting, Genre is up to your own approximation, but hybrids and qualifiers such as those above give you the tools with which to be more specific.

Elements

Sometimes "Attachments." Not all coverage templates include a line for this information, but it's worth mentioning lest you do come across it. Elements are those above-the-line individuals (producers, directors, actors) who, during the development process, have *firmly committed* to working on the film.

Your client/employer might provide you with this information or it might appear on the cover letter that accompanied the script when it was submitted. Agents and producers, especially, will mention any elements they can to help sell the project or attract other talent. It is best to include what role the attached intends to play: Producer, Director, or a character's name.

One thing to watch out for, however, is a person who indicates in his cover letter that a certain actor or director is "interested." The term suggests that this actor or director has a level of enthusiasm for the project but has not officially committed to it. So as not to misrepresent someone's intentions, it is better to leave the person's name out of the Elements section if she is just "interested." If, however, you are compelled to include such an individual, it is advisable to qualify her level of commitment.

You might also come across a coverage template that allows for mention of Elements, but your clients might choose to withhold this information. In this case, they probably want your untainted, wholly objective opinion of the material without the influence of knowing that Jim Carrey is attached to star in it.

All of the above will leave you prepared to fill in the upper third of your top sheet and ready to delve into its more substantive components, starting with the Logline.

The Logline

The logline encapsulates the plot of a script, usually within one to two sentences, though on occasion some might extend to three or four. At first, it will be difficult for you to put a story into such a nutshell, but keep in mind that there is another entire section of coverage dedicated to synopsizing the script. The logline is merely a teaser, or it might provide enough description to tell your client that this project is not for them.

The best way to approach your logline is to consider the first act of the script—the main character, his everyday world or state of mind—and then bring in the first turning point with, perhaps, a dash of its second-act after-effects. Without calling them loglines, I previously provided some examples, some of which you might recognize here:

> A wandering Vietnam vet is unjustly harassed by a small-town Sheriff and forced to flee to the woods, where he fends off local law enforcement and an old mentor. (*First Blood*)

A young, hard-working architect stumbles upon a remote control that enables him to fast forward through or rewind to certain moments in his life. (*Click*)

A ditsy, blond sorority chick goes to Harvard law school to impress her boyfriend. (*Legally Blond*)

A Memphis pimp enters a midlife crisis and decides to lay down a rap demo in the desperate hopes of hitting the big time. (*Hustle & Flow*)

Note that these loglines provide the most important detail(s) about the main character(s), a touch of the conflict they endure, and some suggestion of setting. It's almost like saying, "There's a hero, she's like this, and then she's forced to do something or something happens to her. . . ." with the possible small addition of ". . . causing X to happen." The rest is left to the imagination of the person reading your logline.

It is one thing to see loglines from recognizable films that can be neatly wrapped up in one sentence, but it will also be helpful to read examples for scripts that have not appeared on the screen. (*Please note that, while not produced, the scripts represented by the following loglines describe copyrighted material.*)

A small-town doctor who himself is dying of cancer stumbles across a miracle patient whose body produces cancer-destroying cells. (*The Seventh Cell*, by Jeffrey Whitehead)

In the midst of a 1920s revolt, a young Irish fisherman falls in love with the daughter of a cruel, British landlord. (*Islanders*, screenplay by Casey Jones, based on the novella by Peadar O'Donnell)

A bumbling Mexican-American youth is hired to deliver mysterious cargo south of the border. When he loses his shipment in an impoverished Mexican village, he gets caught in the middle of an escalating tug-of-war to reclaim it. (*Alejandro The Great*)

(See more examples of loglines within the full coverage samples of Appendix A.)

Notice how, in both sets of examples, the loglines immediately dip into who the main character is. Try to refrain from writing loglines that begin with "A story about . . ." or "This is the tale of . . ." We already know it's a story; don't waste the words.

In addition to their usefulness in the evaluation process, loglines provide a handy, commonly accepted sales tool for writers, producers, directors, actors, agents, executives, and others. For example, in a casual setting, a producer might ask a writer, "What's it about?" At that moment, the producer probably would not expect a twenty-minute pitch meeting or even an explanation of its themes, but rather, a logline—a teaser—from which he will either be hooked or not. Before submitting a project to a talent agent or a development executive, a producer might attempt to enthuse her about reading it with the delivery of a snappy logline. With that in mind, creating an effective logline for a project is a strong skill for many in the entertainment industry to know.

Unfortunately, not all scripts will be so well written or marketable that you can easily sum them up with a terse, one-sentence blurb. In such instances, do your best to represent the author's intentions, increase to three or four sentences if truly necessary, and let the rest of the cover page speak for your feelings about the material, starting with the Commercial Potential.

Commercial Potential

In the Commercial Potential segment, like the logline, you will insert another pithy statement. Developing this statement, however, is a far more intricate and weighty task than the logline. Here, you must take a moment to wear the hat of marketers and distributors to offer an informed opinion based not so much on plot as your sense of concept and marketability. Upon assessing commercial potential, you will have to ask yourself a few questions, including: Who is the target audience? Would this story be well received by that audience? Can the material be compared to other films that have already been produced? Might the script thrive in a market additional to theatrical release (i.e., movie theaters)?

Who Is the Target Audience?

To answer this question, return to those target audiences we discussed in the previous section, including: the youth market, eighteen-to-twenty-nine-year-olds, the art house niche, minorities; baby boomers, children, and families. Your judgment will most likely be based on the writing's genre, tone, and themes. For example, is it a comic road movie full of fart jokes, sexual fantasy, and anti-establishment sentiment? Then it could be one for the teen market and/or eighteen-to-twenty-somethings. Is it a gritty, urban drama that speaks out against racial inequality? It could be for the specialty houses, though it might also hope to bring in certain minority groups and cross over to the mainstream.

Unfortunately, it is not always that easy to pinpoint the target audience of a script. The genre may be too hybridized, the tone too uneven, or the theme too ill-defined for you to make heads or tails of the author's intentions. In such cases, you could mention in your Commercial Potential that the script has little or no commercial potential, because there is no identifiable target audience.

Will This Script Be Well Received by That Target Audience?

It is all educated guesswork as to whether material will actually be embraced in the marketplace, though, as William Goldman classically puts it in his *Adventures in the Screen Trade* (Warner Books): "Nobody knows anything." Not only can script readers horrifically over- or underestimate the commercial potential of a screenplay, so do most others in the industry, all the way up the ladder to the most powerful of CEOs who greenlight projects.

Indeed, I remember listening to the president of one major production company reject the script for *Sling Blade* with a simple, "I just don't get it." Soon after, that script went on to earn an Academy Award for Best Adapted Screenplay. *Very few* at any level would have guessed that a gory, Christian-themed story spoken in Latin and Aramaic with no recognizable stars would take its place among the world's highest grossing films ever (*The Passion of the Christ*). Who could have imagined that a "mockumentary" about a Kazakh journalist traveling across America (*Borat*), especially when pitted against two well-hyped family films, would take the top spot at the box office in its opening weekend and go on to earn over a $100 million in its theatrical release? Conversely, studio execs and many others assumed that films such as *Gigli* or *The League of Extraordinary Gentlemen* would do through-the-roof business based on concept and star power, while those projects collapsed into critical and box office disappointments.

These examples, however, are major exceptions. Within the vast ocean of material written for the screen, it is usually possible to make a somewhat educated guess regarding a project's commercial potential. One way to do so is to study history. How have other films of the same genre or of a similar storyline performed at the box office or on television? You might know simply from the publicity a film received whether it crashed or thrived in the market. If you are not positive, you might refer to resources such as IMDbpro.com, BaselineFT, or *Variety* archives to research a film's budget versus its domestic box office gains. If a film recouped its budget in the U.S. ("domestic") box office, then it might be safe to say that it went on to at least break even, if not make some money, taking into account the additional markets of foreign distribution, DVD/video, new media, and television. Know that some films will either match or surpass their domestic box office grosses in overseas markets. (More about ancillary markets and foreign distribution in a moment.) Though you may have to pay for a subscription to some of these resources, it might be worth the expense to be able to access a quick budget figure or box office total as backup to your instincts.

Of course, if the writing itself is poor, then you are safe to assume that there is little commercial potential. Generally, you should subscribe to the idea that if it is not on the page, the quality will not appear on the screen—no matter what megastar or accomplished director is attached to the script. On occasion, however, you might sense some promise in the concept itself, which is worth noting, and indicate that there is potential, pending a rewrite. On the other hand, the fact that the material is well written does not always guarantee healthy box office receipts. For example, a lavish, character-driven period drama might exist as a superb piece of writing but could only appeal to a minute slice of the moviegoing population.

Can This Script Be Compared to Other Popular Scripts or Produced Films?

In a statement of commercial potential, people usually appreciate reference to another produced film. The use of comparison is a good way to convey a lot of information about a script while saying very little. If, for example, you mention that a script has been written in the vein of *Fried Green Tomatoes*, your client will automatically register that this script is character-driven, bittersweet in tone, geared toward an older, female crowd with some crossover potential, and leaning toward low budget. If you were to label a script a rehash of *Battlefield Earth*, one would immediately know that it is a big-budget story full of effects, an ensemble of aliens, unremarkable dialogue, and an unengaging premise that would be doomed at the box office and elsewhere.

Note that you might also do an inverse comparison. In other words, you might deduce that a writer is *trying* to achieve the same effect as a certain successful film and go on to clarify that this particular work doesn't come near that film. Conversely, you could say that a script resembles some box office failure—in premise, character, tone, or what have you—but that this piece of writing demonstrates a marked improvement over that predecessor.

Additionally, you might compare a script to the *style* of works created by a known producer, director, or actor. For example, if you indicate that a script possesses the qualities of a Jim Jarmusch film, one might deduce that it is low-budget, quirky, character-driven, darkly humorous, and possibly ensemble in nature. Or you might say a script is along the lines of a Jerry Bruckheimer film, indicating that it is a big-budget action or adventure story that could become a mainstream crowd-pleaser.

Might the Script Thrive in a Market Additional to or Other Than Theatrical Release?

While multiplex theaters serve mainstream moviegoers of all ages and specialty venues exhibit the foreign, low-budget, and independent films for the art house set, there are additional markets and outlets that you should be aware of as you evaluate a project's commercial potential. Most pictures are now outgrossing their domestic theatrical performance in these areas.

Most notable in recent years is the ascent of the public's appetite for DVDs. Michael Bayer, director of business affairs and legal at Paramount Pictures Worldwide Home Entertainment indicates, "Some studios actually base their decisions as to whether to greenlight a film for theatrical release on what the projected home entertainment revenues will be. There are some who even claim that, as the windows [between theatrical and other release platforms] shrink and home entertainment becomes more prevalent, there could be a day when the real financial indicator of a film's success will be the opening weekend grosses on the Wal-Mart shelf or perhaps even on iTunes, as opposed to the opening weekend box office numbers." Therefore, keep in mind that the emphasis on theatrical release is losing ground to home entertainment outlets. In today's market, a small drama, such as *Requiem for a Dream*, which might not perform so well in theaters, could easily enjoy much higher revenue in its DVD incarnation.

A straight-to-video/DVD film (sometimes labeled as a "B movie"; more frequently labeled a "DVD Premiere" by those marketing them) will probably never play in a movie theater, but a combination of its budget and a few marketable elements will have warranted its appearance in video stores around the world. Such films can be of any genre—anything from Family to Slasher. They range from the studio-financed film that never quite made it into the theaters (*Pontiac Moon*) to children's animated fare (*The Land Before Time* series) to a project produced specifically for a certain market (*Species III*) to stories shot by the kid around the block with his own video camera. Specialty arms of distribution companies exist to market some of these projects, and video retailers do purchase them, because the video/DVD-renting population does consume them. Some studios are even beginning to rethink their release strategies for a film with the intention to premiere select projects on DVD and then examine their potential for theaters.

In your commercial potential statement, you might occasionally recommend a script based on its potential in the "DVD Premiere" market. The screenplay might be deficient in uniqueness and/or writing quality, but a producer or distributor might still be able to sell it to retailers merely with the aid of some marketable imagery on the DVD case, such as the suggestion of sex, violence, a certain star, special effects, or appeal to a niche market.

Video-on-demand, pay-per-view, Internet streaming and downloading, and cellular/mobile technologies are also entering the spotlight in terms of a film's release. According to Bayer, "These technologies and release platforms, as well as others being developed which we cannot yet even fathom, will contribute to the broadly defined 'home entertainment' market's rise as an extremely important, if not the most important, focus of the film industry."

Another market to consider is television, which can be broken down into three subcategories: premium cable, basic cable, and network television. Increasingly, the line has blurred between what qualifies a film for theatrical release and what qualifies it for premium cable outlets such as HBO and Showtime. In fact, some films, such as *Lolita, God and Monsters*, or *The Last Seduction*, have skipped back and forth between the two, initially geared toward television but sent into limited theatrical release after the reviews came in. These pay networks have, in the past, taken risks and acquired better material, consequently attracting more big-name talent. Furthermore, these networks have touted their own originals (although it must be noted that the current trend is leaning away from original material and more toward series, which are more likely to maintain subscriber loyalty). Original titles from premium cable include: *The Girl in the Café, Iron Jawed Angels, Angels in America, Wit*, and *Miss Evers' Boys*. Premium cable films are usually softer, headier, more theme-oriented, or don't have enough star power to open a film theatrically, but are still grittier, more intelligent, or character-oriented than material suitable for the next category: basic cable networks.

This category of networks is usually included in basic cable packages within medium to large metropolitan markets. They include: FX, Sci-Fi, Lifetime, USA, TNT, Hallmark, A&E, and Oxygen. All original content produced by these networks aims to exploit a very specific slice of the mainstream. Hallmark, for example, is geared toward families; Lifetime and Oxygen target mainstream adult women; Sci-Fi speaks for itself; A&E seeks older, educated audiences; and USA, TNT, and FX content is often skewed adult male but can reach out to women as well. Regardless of the focus, the point is that these networks, too, are producing films, and you may end up reading scripts more suitable for one of these niche outlets than for theatrical or premium cable distribution.

To comfortably indicate that a film's commercial potential rests with one of the above, the budget you imagine would have to be low enough (relatively low on effects, locations, star power), the story would have to be soft enough (to appear in anyone's living room per FCC standards), and the target audience specific enough. Some examples of original films produced for or acquired by these networks include: *The Pirates of Silicon Valley* (USA), *The Hunchback* (TNT), *Audrey's Rain* (Hallmark), *Anonymous Rex* (Sci-Fi), and *A Daughter's Conviction* (Lifetime).

The four basic television networks (CBS, ABC, NBC, FOX), on the other hand, will usually produce material for a wider demographic. TV movies, often called MOWs (Movie of the Week), tend to be even softer, slower, more issue-oriented, more melodramatic, and lower in budget than those for the basic cable networks and will aim for the largest possible slice of mainstream television viewers. They might cover topics such as domestic abuse, substance abuse, infidelity, depression, and some high-profile true stories. Titles have ranged from *Bill* to *Martha Behind Bars*. A network might also turn out a disaster flick to correspond with a current theatrical release or an unnerving current event (for example, *Fatal Contact: Bird Flu in America*).

Television movies for the major networks are not nearly as prolific as they used to be, due in part to the advent of the lucrative reality TV market, along with increased competition from the cable networks. Unless you are reading specifically for one of the major networks or its producers, it is seldom that you will come across reading material intentionally written for them. In your commercial potential statement, you might compare material to an MOW, but that will probably translate as showing no potential at all.

One other consideration to keep in mind as you write the Commercial Potential section is that feature films are showing strength in foreign theaters. While the 2005 international market experienced a nominal dip from the robust grosses reported in 2004, the overseas box office could account for 65 percent or more of a film's total theatrical revenue. In 2005, *The Island*, for example, grossed about $125 million internationally, while it did only $12 million on U.S. soil. In 2006, *Mission: Impossible 3* grossed a lower than expected $48 million on its opening weekend, but on international soil it accumulated another $70 million. Generally, it is thought that period epics (*Alexander and Kingdom of Heaven*) and event films (*King Kong and the Harry Potter* films) will do just as well if not better in foreign territories.

The following are some examples of Commercial Potential statements from actual coverage:

> This script is written in the vein of such ensemble pieces as *Happiness* or *Hannah and Her Sisters*, but it's neither edgy nor funny enough to guarantee those crowds.

> With its *Romeo and Juliet* romance, broad action sequences, and fresh setting, this European period piece evinces potential appeal for art house and mainstream audiences alike. Its potential to perform in foreign territories seems especially strong.

> This supernatural story aims for those who liked *Ghost* or *Heart and Souls* but doesn't execute as well as those precedents.

> It reads like an easy NC-17. A grittier *Four Brothers* comes to mind, but a lack of heroic, well-defined pursuits by its characters detracts from any potential. The bleak finish doesn't help, either.

Notice that these examples, like the logline, are written as complete sentences rather than less professional half ideas.

Element Ratings

Not to be confused with "Elements" in the upper third of the cover page, these elements refer to the story basics—often concept, structure, plot, characters, and dialogue. In this segment of the cover sheet, you will offer a qualitative evaluation of each element as directed by your client's template. Usually, the four options are: Poor, Fair, Good, and Excellent. You might be required to write one of these options next to the listed element, though more commonly you will be able to simply X your grade into a prepared grid, leading some to refer to these as "Box Scores" or "Grid Ratings." The following is an example of an element ratings table:

(X)	EXCELLENT	GOOD	FAIR	POOR
CONCEPT		...X...		
STORYLINE				X
CHARACTERS	X			
DIALOGUE		X		

It is common for readers to be on the fence between one grade and the other. In such cases, you should feel free to place one under each grade or one somewhere in between, as depicted in the "Concept" category above.

While the grid method is most often used, some companies will vary slightly by requesting your evaluation on a number scale. Some television studios have their readers apply letter grades to the basic story elements.

It would be easy to read a script and call the dialogue good, the plot fair, the premise poor, and leave it at that. But remember: this cover page is merely an overview of what is to be detailed and supported in the following sections of your coverage. If you mark one element as good or as poor, *be wholly prepared to back up that sentiment in your comments section* (covered in detail in chapter 7).

Story Brief

You won't find this part in every coverage template, but it is worth mentioning in case you do come across it. The Story Brief (or Brief) can best be described as your element ratings written in sentence form. It can be frustrating to a reader if the Brief and Commercial Potential are both required, since the two could overlap; you might find yourself trying to say the same thing in two different ways. In general, the Commercial Potential should focus on concept and marketability alone, whereas your Brief should address the remaining story elements such as tone, theme, plot, structure, dialogue, pace, and character. Naturally, you are not going to be able to cover all of these elements in one or two sentences. You should just concern yourself with the glaringly bad or good aspects of the material. Here are some examples from actual coverage:

> Though the second act could use a little more breathing time and it's a bit cartoonish, the main character is so endearing and the overall storyline is enough fun to warrant consideration.

> Its over-familiar premise, dull plot, and melodramatic tone promise to disappoint.

> Despite the many laughs and a few good twists and turns, large windows of plot become stale, and the final act fails to pay off.

What the Brief amounts to is a thesis statement for your comments section without too much emphasis on commercial considerations. Hence, this section might also be labeled the "Comment Summary." Like the Commercial Potential and Element Ratings, again you will be required to elaborate on your thoughts later in the coverage, so be prepared to back up your statement. Also note that some clients might only ask you for a Brief or Comment Summary without the Commercial Potential. In that case, you will have the flexibility to blend aspects of both marketability and story into one statement.

Budget

Most cover sheet templates will leave space for you to approximate the budget of a script. That is not to say you will have to give it a specific dollar value—usually, you will have to write in or mark off a simple Low, Medium, or High. Haven't had film budgeting experience? Most readers haven't, and no one is going to fault you for calling a budget low when it could be medium, or medium when it could be high. In fact, some films could be produced in both high- and low-budget scenarios. This aspect of the cover page just serves as a loose guide, mainly for executives, producers, managers, and agents.

Roughly speaking, low budgets reach up to about $8 million; medium budgets could range from about $8 to 30 million; and high budgets anything above that. So how do you estimate? Again, it might help you to compare the script to others of a similar genre and/or storyline. What do you know about the budgets for those? Be careful, however. A film that cost $6 million twenty years ago would probably cost more today. On the other hand, thanks to the Digital Age, special effects and other post-production costs can often be remarkably low.

Your best bet will be to base your approximation on instinct more than anything else. Does the script suggest few characters and locations and little to no special effects? It's probably low budget. Would the script require a broad cast of A-List stars, sweeping visual effects, a loaded soundtrack, locations around the globe, and an optimistic studio to bankroll and market it? High budget. If it's somewhere between those two extremes, call it medium.

Regardless of your budget barometer, know that it is not the most important part of coverage. A seasoned producer or executive will probably be able to read your logline and decipher the script's budget range just from that. When writing your coverage, you needn't spend more than a minute deliberating on the projected cost of the film.

The Recommendation (To Be Continued . . .)

Depending on the client and their template, the recommendation might appear on the top sheet and/or it could appear on the back page at the end of your commentary. Arguably the single most important aspect of coverage, this is the part where you say in so many words, "Yes, read this script immediately," or "There's something to this that might make it worth reading," or "Without going any further, recycle this paper and move on to the next one." The recommendation, however, is so very closely linked to your comments that we will save any further discussion on the topic for chapter 7.

6

The Synopsis

To summarize a 120-page screenplay within one or two pages is an art form in its own right. Like coverage itself, the purpose of the synopsis can vary. Often, the synopsis will serve as your client's "Cliff's Notes" for the screenplay so they don't have to read the material themselves. I have worked for many who rarely, if ever, read the screenplay, citing the synopsis as a sufficient tool to familiarize themselves with the story. Okay, you might have something to say about that if you are a screenwriter or if you otherwise represent a project, but that's the way it is in Hollywood, and that frame of mind is one of the major reasons why coverage exists in the first place.

Though less frequently, your synopsis could also be used as a sales tool. Producers, agents, managers, and others might discard the rest of the coverage and simply present the one-page summary to prospective buyers, financiers, and other elements. Additionally, I have seen writers, directors, and producers who, despite knowing the story inside and out and backwards, request a synopsis in their coverage. In these cases, a synopsis by an objective source can help those in search of feedback understand if the story is being projected and perceived the way it was intended to be.

Synopsis Format

The page requirements for a synopsis will vary from client to client, but generally they run between one and two pages, single-spaced. Make sure to establish the desired page range with your client before beginning work. Some might not want to read anything more than half a page at this stage; others could want an in-depth synopsis up to three pages, though anything over two pages is usually considered above and beyond for standard story analysis.

It is also highly recommended that you break up your paragraphs at major story beats. Some professional readers do this very little, if at all, but put yourself in your client's shoes; imagine having to read one long, two-page paragraph. To do some justice to the material you are covering, as well as your own writing style, add some cadence to the synopsis by breaking it up. At the very least, it would be logical to break at the end of each act, as well as during the major points within those acts. Additionally, your writing instincts might tell you to indent at the beginning of each paragraph. It's not entirely right or wrong to do so, but it has evolved into the norm *not* to.

Similar to an actual screenplay, it is customary to put the name of a character in all caps upon first mention in a synopsis and include in parentheses their age or age range. Some readers choose (or are required) to put character names in all caps throughout, intended for the client's quick reference to a certain persona or type.

Technique and Tone

The main challenge is for you to create a synopsis that presents a compact, logical, readable, and smooth representation of the story you have just read. The temptation for beginning script readers is to outline a script scene by scene, event by event, detail by detail, character by character. What happens is that they reach two full pages of synopsis and realize that they've only summarized half the story. Reviewing what you know about structure will help you immensely as you try to extract essential parts of a script to place into your synopsis. After all, within each act there are only so many major beats that you can detail. If, in narrative form, you can sum up the initial universe of the main character and then hit the catalyst, the first turning point, a few key events in Act IIA, the midpoint, and so on, you'll be on your way to a solid synopsis.

It's easy for a client to get lost in the who's who and where's where of a screenplay. Even if you provide a lot of character and setting information in the other sections of your coverage, the synopsis should be able to stand on its own legs. Make sure you guide your client throughout the synopsis by establishing and reestablishing setting and by reminding them who a certain character is, especially if you haven't mentioned him in a while. Transitions such as "Meanwhile, back at the mountain resort . . ." or "Ricky, the short gravedigger from the very beginning of the story . . ." represent perfectly acceptable technique.

As for tone, think of the synopsis as a news article reporting on the script you have read. Unless you have been contracted to put together a sales synopsis with flashy, emphatic language (more about that below), this overview should be a relatively dry account of the plot and characters. It is usually meant to keep the reader not so much entertained as informed about what happens beat by beat. Certainly, you want it to be a smooth, logical read with a sense of story, but matter-of-fact is generally the way you want to go.

One of the biggest mistakes a beginning story analyst will make is to inject her own opinion into the synopsis. Hence, instead of writing, "Cowboy wins the shootout against Snake, uses newfound guts and wisdom to save Nancy from the moving train, and gallops off with her into the sunset," a novice might declare, "*Predictably*, Cowboy wins the shootout with Snake, he *too easily* manages to rescue Nancy from the train, *and the cliché wouldn't be complete* if he didn't ride off into the sunset with her." You will get in your two cents about the script in the top sheet and Comments sections, but here you are most always required to appear objective. Your client may need the synopsis for purposes other than your own read of the story. Furthermore, your client should be given the option to disagree with your opinion based on the hard information he gathers from your synopsis alone.

For samples of standard synopses, see the coverage examples in Appendix A.

Sales and the One-Pager

In the case of standard coverage, you usually have the leeway to summarize the material over the span of about two pages. Difficult as that is, you may come across a situation where it is imperative that you limit the synopsis to a page or less. This situation is often for sales purposes, in which, for example, a producer wants a sales agent to grasp the essential marketing points of the story or a writer wants to offer a producer or executive a quick taste. (Those of you who are also writers might especially want to learn this aspect of coverage.) Here, you will surely draw up a more subjective take on the material with more inspiring language. Suddenly, a sentence such as, "The sailors suffer a massive storm and must set aside their differences to survive it," might become: "The sailors are overwhelmed by an epic tempest and opt to shed their differences in order to band together in the battle of their lives." A bit of your own voice will surface in such a synopsis, but whether you sincerely enjoyed the material or not, it will be your job to represent the story in a positive light—as something unique, taut, and marketable.

For other clients, a one-pager may simply be all the information the client wants to sort through at the moment. Either way—sales or informational—it becomes a real nip and tuck to compress 120 pages of screenplay into a page of summary. Do your best to relate only the very core of the script—that is, the central premise and main journey of the protagonist. Subplot may warrant a few sentences, but a page is not a lot of space, and you will have to stay focused. A series of adventures or character detours may have to be boiled down to an attractive list. For example, if you were writing standard coverage for a script in which the bulk of Act IIB depicts a male and female hero ascending a skyscraper to rescue hostages, you might dedicate a couple of small paragraphs to elaborate on the action and character dynamics. In a one-pager, however, you could be forced to wrap up the main action with a simple: "Working through their sexually charged banter, our heroes execute a series of computer hacks, elevator shaft climbs, vent crawls, and explosive rigs to reach the top floor of the Corporation's building, where the hostages are being detained."

Especially in the case of sales coverage, you might be asked to hold back on the ending. In order to intrigue a prospective buyer, your client might not want to give it away. Hence, you would set up the story by outlining acts one and a good part of two and then leave act three to the imagination. For example, if you read a script about a group of college students in a school-sponsored drama competition, the concluding couple of sentences might read: "What unfolds is a semester of truth, tragedy, and absurd theatrics. Art begins to blur with reality as this unwieldy production group tries to pull together the performance of their lives in time for the big night that will decide it all. . . ." This approach is also comparable to the language you read on the back of a DVD case. Simplified as they are, note how they, too, tempt the reader's imagination. Look at the back of a *Collateral* DVD, for example, which wraps up the story with: "Now, Max has to transport Vincent on his next job—one night, five stops, five hits and a getaway. And after this fateful night, neither man will ever be the same again. Tonight everything is changing. . . ." (*Collateral*, Dreamworks Home Entertainment, 2004).

When Scripts Go Bad

It is relatively easy, sometimes refreshing, to synopsize a tight, well-written script. The writer will have done all the work for you by hitting all of the plot points just so, paying off everything, and avoiding excess characters and dialogue. The synopsis all but lands on your lap. On the other hand, perhaps the trickiest thing you will have to do when you write coverage is to synopsize a convoluted or nonsensical story. You will have many days when, among a stack of poorly written scripts, there will also sit that truly abominable one. Count on it. You know—handwritten, with a second act that begins on page sixty-two, gaping plot holes, one melodramatic soliloquy after the next, no clear protagonist, caught between a musical and a sci-fi drama, and the list goes on. Here, you will have to maintain added restraint so as not to inject your distaste into the plot summary. The question becomes: How do I synopsize a story that isn't a story? When you can't make heads or tails of the author's intentions, your blood pressure will probably rise a few notches as you attempt to untangle such a dizzying puzzle. But hey, it will have to be done; this is what you're getting paid for.

As you construct your synopsis on such material, you will begin to feel like you're relating the story how it *should* be told. You might even feel as though you're rewriting the script altogether while you clarify for your employer what doesn't make sense to you. Here, you can only do your best to create a smooth, logical representation of the story. Again, the temptation may be to include every detail, since you're not sure which details are truly important. If you have to, pull out those details that are most important or intriguing *to you*, and run with it. Standard coverage or otherwise, try to reduce the story to one page of synopsis and then move forward with the rest of your work. If the material is truly that bad, then in all likelihood, you will not be faulted for including some information instead of other or for stretching some events to make for a more logical synopsis.

Synopsizing Other Forms

Everything presented thus far is in relation to reviewing a screenplay. You might, however, be assigned to cover a book, manuscript, play, treatment, or even an article. Given their wide variation in length and attention to detail, books and manuscripts will often warrant a slightly longer synopsis. Don't hesitate to push a book synopsis over the two-page mark into three or even four, if necessary. Readers are usually compensated for the extra work it requires to read and cover a book. While roughly equal in length to a screenplay, a play could go two ways: either not much story to summarize or far more intricacies than one would find in a narrative for the big screen. Regardless, the synopsis for a play should in most cases fall within the two-page limit.

A treatment, which serves as a screenplay proposal in the form of a five- to forty-page narrative, is an extended synopsis in itself. Most clients won't ask a reader to synopsize a treatment, but if it happens, somewhere between a half and a full page of synopsis would be considered acceptable. Likewise, you will rarely if ever be asked to synopsize a newspaper or magazine article. Rather, you will be handed treatments and articles for commentary alone.

7

Comments

You have scratched the surface with your cover page and you have summarized the story in your synopsis. Now it is time to get your hands dirty and evaluate the material you are covering. Here, you have the client's ear; you are given the stage to express your opinion. To do so, you will have to draw upon the myriad story elements discussed in Section I and explain why you feel some of them work very well, not at all, or somewhere in the middle. From the comments segment, your clients might determine how to rewrite the material, what elements they can use to sell it, or reasons why they shouldn't bother reading it at all. While writing your evaluation, you will wear a variety of hats, including that of the critic, development executive, producer, agent, and marketing specialist.

Comments Format

Much of the formatting for your comments will correspond to that of your synopsis. One to two single-spaced pages are standard for full coverage, though some clients may only contract you for a half page or even a few sentences. If someone requests *more* than two pages of comments, then you're dabbling with full-fledged "story notes" or "development notes." This mode of feedback is an extended form of coverage, and you should request to be compensated accordingly. (More about development notes later.) Again, confirm all page specifications with your client before you accept the job and begin reading.

Similar to the synopsis, your commentary should be divided into paragraphs. It would be logical to break at each new main idea about a certain story element. Whether to indent the beginning of each new paragraph is your choice, but it's not entirely necessary.

Content and "The Four Types"

When formulating your commentary, approach it like the English papers you used to write or pattern it after film critiques you have read. Begin with a thesis sentence or paragraph, elaborate over the course of a few more paragraphs, and wrap it up with a concluding statement or two. There will be many occasions when you feel you could earn a doctoral degree explaining why a certain script works or doesn't work. But remember, in coverage you are not expected to go beyond two pages of thought. Certainly, you could work from a checklist of plot, structure, character, format, theme, tone, pace, believability, and so forth. In fact, I encourage this practice to keep you focused and vigilant as you read the script and draft your comments. (See Appendix E for a detailed checklist.) In the end, however, there is not enough room in coverage for you to address them all point by point. Fortunately, some of those elements will jump out of a script more than others. When penning your thoughts, try to expound on those glaringly bad, good, or somewhat promising items.

As in any piece of writing, it is also important to remember to back up your opinion with specific examples. If you are mentioning weak dialogue, add in a quote or two. If you are pointing out tone shift, indicate how and where in the script it happens. If you are applauding strong structure, take us through it act by act (albeit, briefly). No one is going to take your word for it if you simply say that the plot is predictable and move on. You will have to elaborate on such a statement. Using page numbers to correspond to your examples won't always be necessary or applicable, but it is a good idea to insert them when possible.

One mistake readers will make is to flesh out their comments section and forget that they have already completed a cover page with an opinion on it. Therefore, clients could be aggravated or confused when they come across comments that differ significantly from, say, the Commercial Potential or Comment Summary on the first page. Make sure that your evaluation lies in-sync with your top sheet. Do not praise a script's commercial prospects on the cover page and then bash the material in your comments section or don't apply a "fair" rating to the storyline in your elements grid and then extol the plot's virtues in your commentary. Keep in mind that your top sheet represents an overview of all that is to come within the rest of the coverage.

These rules aside, your commentary need not always derive from a fixed mindset. In other words, you could have to alter your own tone, or even your opinion, to suit different clients' needs and tastes. At times, the client might flat-out ask you to skew your thoughts in a certain way for certain purposes (this rare situation will be discussed in a moment), but more often it's a matter of your own intuition regarding the client's relationship with the material. You might say there are four different categories of coverage that could affect the content and angle of your comments. To better understand these various mindsets, let's coin the four coverage types as follows: *standard, constructive, political,* and *sales.*

Standard Coverage

The most common of these categories, standard coverage, is as it sounds: basic or no-frills. It is coverage in its purist, if driest, form and is used mainly by studios and other companies, great and small, that are besieged daily by script submissions. Having never seen the script before, your client will simply want to know if he should read anything more past your own analysis. Hence, you will read the script for the client and just tell it like you see it. If you think it is worth a look, you will say so and explain for reasons x, y, and z. If you think it's not worth the crud under your fingernails, you will also express this in so many words.

This type of coverage will likely be seen by the client only and used for in-house purposes. You can be blunt, but you should always temper your language so as not to sound too abrasive. Even in this most straightforward form of coverage, *you never know in whose hands it will land.* I found myself covering one particularly poor script for a major company, but my instincts told me to hold back on a complete trashfest. Only after I had turned in my report did I learn for whom this evaluation was intended: the *father* of the company's president. Imagine if I had let loose on this writer's work with all the true distaste I was feeling. The insults would surely have gotten back to my somewhat protective and proud employer, and that could have been the end of that. Instead, I had clearly and logically explained my perception of the material with specific examples and little hyperbole, and all walked away satisfied. There is a way to be up front about your opinion without throwing unprofessional insults into your report.

Consider standard coverage to be your default. If you are not sure who your target is, then your best bet is to go with this form.

Constructive Coverage

If there is typically some bite to your critiquing sense, then you will want to tone it down a notch for constructive coverage. The people reading this type of analysis will likely be involved intimately with the script you have just read. Constructive coverage is intended for those entities who know the material quite well (e.g., the writer or a producer) but have become too attached to it to formulate an objective blueprint for a rewrite. As in standard coverage, you will highlight the notably good and the markedly poor elements of the script, but then you will take it a step further and, as the name suggests, supply constructive suggestions for fixing them. It will require some creativity on your part. Pretend you're the author's writing partner and it's your turn to take a crack at the script. How would you improve it?

It is by far more difficult to encapsulate this type of commentary within two pages, as the temptation may be to walk the client through major surgery on the material. (Again, extensive rewrite suggestions come in the form of "development notes," a different form of feedback for which you are not being paid.) If the script is especially poor, stick to general recommendations (e.g., "Consider slashing the volume of dialogue down by a third" or "It is recommended that a rewrite address the lack of an identifiable protagonist.") If you get lucky and come across halfway decent material, then go on to add some specific creative direction to the client's rewrite process. For example, think about new events you would like to see happen, what characters you would like to see more or less of, how you would rework the structure act by act, what you would change to make it less predictable.

In these first two coverage types—standard and constructive—the goal and language may differ, but you will submit a forthright opinion for both. Not quite so for the following, less common, categories.

Political Coverage

Once, I was working for a studio and my supervisor asked me to get a script evaluated for her—a certain pet project that she desperately wanted the company's money and marketing people to embrace. She told me point-blank, "Make sure the coverage comes in favorable." Personally, I thought the script was mediocre. It certainly wasn't worth investing millions. Still, this request came from the individual who hired me, and I had a job to do. So, I pulled one of my best readers aside, gave him the lowdown, and coined what I call "political coverage." The next day, this reader returned coverage to me that gushed about the script's crisp dialogue, unique concept, tight structure, tremendous commercial potential, and so on. Off the record, he thought the script was horrible.

Feel a little squeamish about writing contrary to your true feelings? It is hardly every day you will be asked to do so, but you should be prepared for it to happen at some point in your career. Indeed, political coverage presents a bit of a dilemma. If you agree to write it, then someone higher up than your employer might read it and could fundamentally disagree with your opinion and see to it that your services are never used again. On the other hand, it is not in your best interest to make waves with the person who hired you.

There is a safe way to approach political coverage. If you are told to construct a glowing evaluation for a script that just doesn't do it for you, first, accomplish what has been asked of you: find those aspects that do have a modicum of potential and inflate their worth and positive effect. Every script, no matter how poor, will have at least a pinch of redeeming value. It could be a needle in a haystack, but trust me, it's in there somewhere. (Well . . . it *has* to be, in this case.) Then, to cover yourself, turn to constructive coverage. It's okay to point out an item or two that doesn't work, but go on to qualify your statements with a backpedaling. ("Nonetheless, these faults represent relatively easy fixes that can be cleaned up in a quick polish by doing *x*, *y*, and *z*.") As you can see, there's a lot of praise in there, a little bit of criticism to appease those detractors, and everyone walks away somewhat comfortably. (You might also petition the use of an alias instead of your true name on the top sheet.)

Appalled by what I have implied? Then don't quit your day job. It's not me—it's the business of making movies, and either you want to play or you don't. Incidentally, that mediocre script I was just telling you about? It never got made. But no one was fired because of it, either.

Sales Coverage

The target for sales coverage could be a prospective investor, a sales agent, producer, or even an actor or director who has taken an interest. Sales coverage usually relies on an effusive synopsis rather than feedback in a comments section (positive or otherwise). If you were required to write a comments section for sales coverage, it might become a similar scenario to political coverage; evaluate some material that you despise in a positive light. For sales coverage, however, you can assume more concern about the bottom line. Hence, comments about story elements might take a backseat to those emphasizing return on investment, target audience, marketability, casting potential, and visual possibilities.

More about Style

As you read more and more scripts, you will inevitably develop your own style of writing coverage. An individual voice is encouraged to some extent. Keep your comments interesting for both your client and yourself by dabbling with rich, descriptive terms, such as a "syrupy" tone, a "diaphanous" plot, or a "Furibund" pace. It's not out of the question to mold your comments with a hint of informality. You might use contractions (he's, she's, it's) or an occasional sense of humor. You might even take cues from the snappy language of magazine writers and film critics.

Still, as a rule, try not to bring yourself into it *too* much. Remember that these comments are not so much about you as the material itself. If it becomes about "I" this and "me" that, you are likely to lose the appearance of professional objectivity. Your client (or whomever he shows your evaluation to) could easily rationalize, "Well that's one person's opinion, and this person doesn't know what she's talking about." It is, however, considered appropriate to use the royal "we" or "us" (e.g., "We never receive a sense of urgency" or "The author delivers us a magnificent twist by revealing Ken to be the killer"). One can also utilize "one." For example, "One never grasps the point of the Laura/Jasmine subplot." All of which keeps it more professional, almost subconsciously draws your client into the evaluation, and prevents you from stepping too far into the report as unwelcome company.

At a Loss for Words

If you write coverage, then you qualify as a certain brand of writer, too, which unfortunately makes you susceptible to writer's block. At times, I have found myself seventy pages into a script and still wondering what the heck I'm going to say about it. The temptation is to begin stressing over it, forcing ideas, even to waste time backtracking through the script in the hopes of gaining new inspiration. You begin to worry so much about not having anything to write by your deadline that it snowballs into a paralyzing, self-fulfilling prophecy.

My advice to you in such a situation: *Finish reading the script at all costs.* Often, we don't receive a clear picture of the author's intentions until the third act. The way in which a script wraps up can lead to oodles of comment fodder: the tone shifts or it remains consistent; the plot hole is addressed or it is left wide open; the character completes her arc or she doesn't; the climactic ending is predictable or you never saw it coming. You might be deep into the script, but there still may be a twist or two lurking that could make or break the story. In fact, I would refrain from drawing any conclusions about the material until you finish reading. You might have begun to scribble pages of thoughts only to have them neutralized by a half page of events later down the road.

Furthermore, everyone has an opinion. If you dig deep enough, your gut reaction to the script is in there somewhere; expressing that reaction is usually the best way to go. When you finish reading a script, imagine you are walking out of the movie theater after having seen this film, and your friend asks you, "Did you like it?" I doubt you would remain silent. Rather you will answer first with an instinctive, "Yes, I liked it a lot," "No, I hated it," "It was just okay," or "I thought it was fairly good but lacking in a couple of areas." That initial response will, in effect, become the thesis statement for your comments. All you have to do from there is back up the gut response with a few examples using the critiquing vocabulary you already know.

Commenting on Other Forms

While your synopsis for a book or manuscript may run a little longer than a standard script synopsis, there is no reason why your comments should. When commenting on a book, *keep in mind that you are not critiquing the book itself but the material's adaptability into a feature film or TV movie.* How do you know? An adaptable book—fiction or otherwise—will have many of the same elements that a good screenplay does: an engaging and unpredictable plot; a clear structure and sense of character arc; universally appealing themes; a unique premise. Naturally, authors of books have the luxury of including far more complexity than a screen version would allow. It's up to you to step away from those details and decide if the core storyline and themes could be extracted, perhaps reconfigured, to create appealing *visual* entertainment. One aspect you don't need to address is dialogue. Although you might mention its adaptation potential, it is generally understood that speech in a book will not translate well onto the screen and will inevitably be reworked by a screenwriter from the ground up.

As for the treatment, short story, or article, you will have to wear a number of hats to conclude whether the writing can be expanded into a strong, satisfying, visual screenplay or teleplay with all the trimmings. Is it a marketable premise with great storytelling potential and engaging characters? Is structure inherent in the piece or would it have to be designed or redesigned by the screenwriter? You might even go so far as to make suggestions based on how you imagine the subject matter in script form.

Moment of Truth: The Recommendation

After the script has been read, the top sheet constructed, and the story summarized and evaluated, this is what it all comes down to. Your Recommendation expressed in a word or two might have the power to plummet someone into deep depression or launch him into euphoria; it could relegate him to obscurity or catapult him into instant fame; it could ignite a megafranchise or bring years of toil to a dead end; it could send shockwaves throughout the industry or amount to a mere blip intended for the circular file. You must know that, as the gatekeeper, a script reader is indeed handed a lot of power, and it is the Recommendation that serves as the reader's final stamp of approval or rejection. In terms of format, the Recommendation might appear on the top sheet or at the beginning or end of your Comments section. Regardless of placement, your client—no matter who it is—will invariably gravitate toward your Recommendation before any other part of the coverage.

The standard three recommendations have evolved into *Recommend, Consider*, and *Pass*. Here is a loose guideline for each:

> *Recommend*: Not to be doled out liberally. You would apply this recommendation to a script that lies within the top 2 to 5 percent of all those you have read or *will ever read*. My personal test is to ask myself: "If I had the money, would I confidently invest it in this project?" When you stamp a script with a "Recommend," you should believe in it with your heart and soul as a sure thing to become a critical and/or financial success.

> *Consider*: In other words, you give it a big "Maybe" or "Consider for Development." Perhaps the premise is too appealing to completely pass up, though the actual execution

is in need of work. Or the script is quite well written, though you're not entirely convinced it can make money. Or you're hopelessly ambivalent about the whole thing. This is your way of telling your client that it's not time to celebrate, but that there is some value here that could make it worth their time to investigate. A Consider project should lie approximately within the top 5 to 10 percent of all those you have read or ever will read.

Pass: Learn how to spell it. Some development folks call it a "Pasadena." The majority of scripts you read will unfortunately warrant this recommendation. This isn't my opinion, mind you, but a known fact in the business. If you were to visit any story department at any studio or agency and inventoried "Pass" coverage versus other, I guarantee you that the former would likely amount to at least 95 percent of all the reports. By stamping "Pass," you are saying to your client, "No, I would not recommend your spending any more time or money on this project." It's a difficult thing to do at first, knowing that you are urging the door closed on this piece of writing. But keep in mind that there are tens of thousands of scripts and script ideas out there and that your client's resources are finite. If this story doesn't resonate as a complete package for you or if it doesn't have the potential to blossom into such, then it behooves you to label it a "Pass" and move on to the next.

While these three are the standard, I have also come across a number of permutations, including a simple *Yes* for Recommend, *Maybe* for Consider, and *No* for Pass. Some recommendations also allow for some gray area. *Qualified Pass* might be used by a reader who regrets or hesitates to assign a Pass. Although you can't confidently recommend the material, you might see some merit in the project and use a Qualified Pass to laud its noble thoughts or themes, an original (but unmarketable) premise, well-written segments, or some other noteworthy quality. A little further along the continuum, you might offer a *Slight Consider* or *Weak Consider*, which serve as a sort of Honorable Mention. Beyond Consider and just short of Recommend, I've seen readers use a *Strong Consider*.

In the end, it is up to your client whether you can employ such variations. Some who are seeking feedback on one of their own projects may appreciate these levels as an equivalent of a plus or minus in a letter grade. Others may insist that you strictly adhere to Pass/Consider/Recommend. Even if not, it's a better way to go to provide your client with a clear, confident recommendation. Chances are, you have been hired to provide a black-and-white "Yes, this script should be considered" or "No, this script should not be considered." Other gradations may make the decision process more difficult for your client than they wish it to be. Use these "tweeners" sparingly.

Most important, as your comments and top sheet should be in synch with each other, so should your project recommendation be with the other two. For example, be careful not to stamp a Pass on a script that you've just praised in your comments and/or cover page; refrain from a Strong Consider after you've prescribed a major rewrite elsewhere in the coverage.

Recommending the Writer

Beyond your Project Recommendation, there is a second grade that might be requested by your client: the Writer Recommendation. As indicated here, you are not evaluating the work itself, but rather the individual(s) who created it. This component can seem absurd at times. After all, how can you separate the writer from the material when this particular piece is all you know of that writer? The instinct is valid, and in most cases your Writer Recommendation should simply match that of the script. If you give a script a Pass, it would make perfect sense to assign the same sentiment to the person who wrote it;

an author who pens Recommend material certainly warrants a similar stamp of approval.

The script and writer recommendations, however, may differ slightly in the following situations: 1) You see fair to great potential in the concept and/or overall storyline of the script and think your client should pursue it but with a different writer on board, given the particularly weak execution of this particular draft; or 2) You think the writer is writing on a fair to excellent level, but you don't hold high hopes for the script itself in the marketplace.

Still, writer and material recommendations are usually linked to a degree—at the very least, your two recommendations should rest near each other on the continuum. For example, it would be far more common and acceptable to give a script a Pass and a writer a Qualified Pass (or Slight Consider) than to give the script a Pass and the writer a Recommend.

The one case in which the Writer Recommendation takes absolute precedence over the Project Recommendation is in the writing sample. A producer or director might be seeking a screenwriter to create a draft of a script and will shop for a good match by viewing work samples from a number of writers. In these instances, the Project Recommendation might not even apply, as these samples may already have been optioned, purchased, or produced by an outside party. Commercial potential becomes less of an issue, as well. When covering the writing sample, not only will the Writer Recommendation be highlighted, but the comments section should be geared more toward the individual writer's strengths, weaknesses, and overall voice. In your comments, you might even include a comparison or general impression stemming from other works that you have read (or viewed) by that writer.

8

The Character Breakdown

A talent agent wants to know what roles lie in a script for her various clients. A studio wants to give its casting department a head start as they ramp up production for a certain project. An independent producer is working without a casting director as he tries to secure funds for a certain script, and he wants agents, prospective financiers, and the director to have a general sense of the key roles.

These are but a few reasons why a client might ask you to include a Character Breakdown in your coverage. Not all coverage templates will call for this component, but it's an important one to know. For the Character Breakdown, you will don the hat of the casting director by identifying the principal roles in the piece and describing each with specifics, including the following:

Name: Use a full name if available.

Age: Identify not the character's specific age but the range in which an actor might fall to play the part.

Race and/or ethnicity: Use your judgment and the description provided by the writer. Whatever is considered politically correct at the time will do.

Type: The level of the character's involvement and the gender (e.g., Leading Female; Supporting Male).

Description: The character in a nutshell, four sentences maximum. Talk about hang-ups, weaknesses, flaws, habits, notable physical features, hopes, and fears in addition to role in the story. You might also mention the end point of the character's arc. Your thoughts may be terse.

Depending on the scope of the story, a Character Breakdown might include up to fifteen personae or as few as one or two. Usually, it's somewhere right in the middle. Note that the entire cast of a script need not be included. If a character appears or is mentioned in twenty or more pages, consider entering them into the breakdown. The following is an example:

ROLE	TYPE	AGE	ETHNICITY	DESCRIPTION
MARTIN "DANTE" POLLACK	Leading Male	40–50	Jewish/ Italian- American hybrid	A modern-day, obsessive-compulsive, curmudgeonly hunchback. Owns a dry cleaning store but critiques roller coasters on the side. Bored with life and tries to change it, only to have things backfire on him.
NATALIE	Leading Female	25–35	Caucasian	A young, capricious beauty; the symbol of Dante's desires. But hidden beneath her happy-go-lucky veneer is the pain of addiction and abuse.
JOANNE	Supporting Female	40–50	Caucasian	A local massage therapist who, after years of friendship with Dante, has developed the hots for him. A bit clingy, gossipy, and frumpy, but she learns how to make a life for herself.
TERRY	Supporting Female	30–40	Caucasian/ British	Tough cookie who shows up in the third act. Like Dante, she obsesses about Natalie. Suffers from addiction problems of her own, but does the right thing for everybody in the end.
MARK	Supporting Male	30–50	Caucasian/ British	Tough Brit who runs the coffee shop downstairs from Natalie's place. One of Natalie's guardian angels.

While a chart format such as the one on the previous page is the most common for a Character Breakdown, you might simply be asked to provide a short paragraph for each character.

––––––––––––

By learning story analysis essentials from title page to recommendation, you have familiarized yourself with the tools of the trade. At this point, however, I can hear you muttering to yourself, "This is all well and good, but how does anyone make any money doing it?" Putting the instrument of coverage to use for practical, money-making purposes is the topic of the next and final section.

SECTION III
The Business

GETTING THE WORK, KEEPING IT, AND USING IT TO FORWARD YOUR CAREER

A s with any skill and job search, pursuing the business side of story analysis is going to require a bit of practice and a lot of patience. And before the practice and patience part—whether your goal is to read for supplement, stop gap, stepping stone, and/or as full-time professional—you will have to ensure that you have some basics in place:

1. *Equipment.* You will need a computer with sufficient memory and Internet access. The days of faxing, mailing, and messengering scripts are quickly coming to a close; the e-mailing of scripts is developing into the norm. More about this later, but if it won't put you too far in debt, I highly recommend investing in a laptop and wireless Internet. The world of Wi-Fi will give you the flexibility to receive scripts, read them, and send in your report from anywhere—a comfy rocking chair, a couch, the bathroom floor, coffee shop, airplane, whatever floats your boat. This leads us to the next basic. . . .

2. *Work area.* You must have a comfortable, quiet space in which to work, away from distractions. To get through a script in one sitting usually requires discipline when the phone, fridge, dog, baby, CNN, doorbell, e-mail, M&Ms, and many other fancies are calling your name. It doesn't matter if you intend to be a professional story analyst, an intern, assistant,

or junior executive—if you have to read a screenplay on the job, make sure you have a space where you can lock the door and turn off the phone so that the reading and evaluation process doesn't take you longer than need be. It might be at home or, if you're lucky, a secluded space away from your residence that you can call an office. Which brings up the final necessity. . . .

3. *Time*. Whether you are in practice mode or doing it for remuneration, script coverage requires time. If it's a well-written script and you're getting the hang of it, it might only take an hour to an hour and a half to read and another hour to cover. The *worst* of scripts, however, might tax you for as long as three hours to read, another hour to piece together a lucid story synopsis, another hour to adequately bash it in your comments, and a few more seconds to toss the script in the trash. The type of coverage you are writing might also bear influence on the time commitment. Standard coverage, for example, is just a functional overview. Given your client won't be so much on the lookout for extreme detail, it probably won't occupy as much time as, say, constructive coverage—especially for a script that requires heaps of rewriting (thus, your own creative input). For each script, then, be able to set aside three to five hours of total work time, though it could take as long as five to six hours if you're new to this. If it gets to the point where you can do it in less time, all the better! But it would be unwise to sacrifice quality in doing so.

With your needs for equipment, space, and time addressed, you are ready to explore two final concerns quite relevant to the world of story analysis: getting work and maintaining it.

9

Getting Work

Obviously, if you want to get paid as a professional story analyst or leverage your coverage savvy to boost your career, you will need to be able to prove your skill to yourself and to others. Try to establish a rhythm and style now, so that when the work does come in, you're able to hit the ground running. Even if becoming a full-time professional script reader is not your objective, there is a lot to be gained from practicing your technique. Refined story sense, knowledge of certain writers, appreciation of certain styles, and, of course, coverage samples will all help you converse intelligently in that interview for assistant, production assistant, intern, story editor, or development exec.

Step One: Practice

By practice, I do not mean downloading or purchasing a script for a film that has already been made. As someone who hires readers, I shy away from those coverage samples that analyze scripts from produced works. That's cheating as far as I'm concerned. Yes, I'm sure you saw *Crash* and liked it, too (or maybe you didn't like it). But how much time have you had to think about it, and how many reviews did you read before you covered the script? When reading a film that has been made, your opinion has already been tainted by outside influences. For better or worse, you already know how to visualize it on screen, you know what kind of box office it raked in, you know what the critics and public have said about it. You also know that there's something redeemable about the material (at least in someone's eyes), since it has survived a number of gatekeepers to reach the screen or video store. Instead, I strongly urge you to simulate a real work situation in which chances are you will never have seen nor heard of your assignments; you will not always receive scripts in your favorite genre; and you will have only a few days or hours—not weeks or months—in which to formulate an opinion.

It should be easier than you think to locate a few scripts for your practice runs. First, you will inevitably know someone—or someone who has a friend or uncle or grandmother—who has written a screenplay. Ask around. By borrowing someone's script, you might be able to arrange for some mutual benefit; you get your guinea pig and they get some critique. For those of you who are aspiring screenwriters, your classes, workshops, or writers groups might provide a fertile ground for material to cover. Be careful though: if a particular script comes directly from the writer or friend/family of the writer, that person must be able to accept your criticism. (You might be wise to try your hand at constructive coverage on that one.)

There are also script exchanges on the Web where writers who are hungry for feedback post their material for critiquing. One of the most popular of these sites is Kevin Spacey's Triggerstreet.com. Here, screenwriters upload their material for review, but only after they themselves critique a certain number of scripts by other authors. Even if you haven't written any screenplays yourself, I am sure that community would embrace an extra set of eyes to evaluate their long list of scripts online. And writers don't always receive full coverage from that system, so your relatively detailed look at their script would probably be welcome. (See some more ideas in Appendix C.)

Furthermore, writing professors and workshop instructors are bound to have mounds of nascent material at their fingertips—be it screenplays, novels, or short stories. If you don't know any such mentors, call a film, TV, and/or writing department at a school near you and introduce yourself. Let them know your intention to practice coverage on a few unknown scripts. You might be asked to (or offer to) sign something so that the teacher can maintain a record of whose hands the material has touched. But again, the situation could turn into one of mutual benefit, as that person—instructor or student—might appreciate someone else's perspective.

Taking Notes

Your first few practice runs are going to be the most difficult, given you will be thinking and writing in a way that is relatively new to you. One major temptation will be to jot several notes per page as you go. Everyone's process is different, and some established readers may in fact employ that technique, but I recommend against it. I remember starting that way myself. I would read a page or two and then type in a paragraph of synopsis. Then, I would go on to scribble a few ideas in anticipation of my comments section. Using that method, however, I realized that I was wasting time on events in the story that later fizzled into insignificance—events that didn't belong in a summary. I also found myself drawing premature conclusions about the material or the writer, as that opinion would often shift later in the script when new information was revealed. As a result, my coverage was running too long and the entire process was occupying more time than it should have.

As a remedy, I began to implement a different approach. While reading, I would jot down no more than a few major beats for my synopsis—mainly the turning points, midpoint, and a few others, if necessary (e.g., "Jimmy embarks on quest"; "Jimmy gets lost in the lair"). By writing these main ideas, you will find yourself at the end of a script with a simple map or blue print for quick, easy reference without having wasted all that time elaborating on unimportant details. And by referring to these brief points, you will be surprised by how many in-between details you do remember to help you complete the summary. Any of those details that you can't remember probably don't warrant mention in a brief synopsis.

As for comments, I stopped drawing conclusions or taking notes, except for a few mental ones, until at least a few pages into the third act. Sure, there might still be a twist or two in store—hence, you might reserve final thoughts regarding predictability until the very end—but by then you should have a pretty good idea of a character's arc, the dialogue, the structure, tone, and so forth.

In sum, the message here is to simplify your reading experience—starting with your earliest practice runs—by minimizing the notes you take along the way. At first, the fear of not having anything to say might overwhelm you, but try giving your memory and intuition the benefit of the doubt, and see what happens.

Develop Your Portfolio

After a sufficient number of practice runs, you should be able to go on to this next step. It's as easy as this: take what you consider to be your five best coverage samples and have them readily available to submit to a prospective client or employer. Make sure that these samples are diverse in both genre and your opinion of the material. Also make sure that they are indeed your five best samples, which might entail having an honest and experienced friend read through them with a bit of editing to follow.

On a legal note, it is generally understood that your coverage samples represent evaluations of copyrighted and/or Writers Guild of America registered material. Still, if possible, you might offer the courtesy of requesting permission (preferably in writing) to use coverage of someone else's material for your "portfolio." If the script's rights belong to the author, get permission from the author; if the writing has been optioned or purchased by some third party, seek permission from them. Since they are samples and will only be seen by a few, chances are slim that your comments (especially negative ones) about a script will affect its chances of success on the market. Still, an unexpected lawsuit could significantly divert your efforts in the story analysis business.

Usually, a prospective client will only ask for one or two samples—perhaps one script you liked and one you didn't. It might be a good idea, however, to include in your portfolio coverage of a script that you thought was somewhere in the middle—one sample that will display your ability to pick out both strengths and weaknesses within one piece of writing. Also consider a sample that is particularly constructive in tone. Many clients will want to know that you come with fresh, creative ideas to help them *fix* screenplays, not just pass on or recommend them. When asked for coverage samples, it is also up to your own intuition to gauge the client's or company's tastes. If the client mainly directs action movies, then give him action coverage. If a company produces small, quirky art house films, produce some coverage for that genre.

To your portfolio of five or so samples, add a simple business card, and believe it or not, you are ready to label yourself a professional story analyst. Of course, you will need to build a résumé next.

Who's Hiring and How to Reach Them
First, let's talk about the obvious targets: production/development companies, studios, agencies, management companies. Large and small, these entities are sure to be receiving volumes of submissions and will likely have at least one story analyst on call, if not a staff of them. How do you get your foot in those doors? Well, for one thing, there are job lists—the most famous being the UTA (United Talent Agency) job list. This one, however, can be quite elusive. To get your hands on it, you will have to ask around—often within New York and L.A. industry circles—in the hopes that someone can forward it to you when they receive it. You might have more luck with more accessible, strictly Web-based job lists such as craigslist.org (especially the New York and L.A. sections) or entertainmentcareers.net. For the truly

determined, you might consider the Hollywood Creative Directory, which lists contact information for most every established production company in the business. Try e-mailing, mailing, or faxing a query letter with an offer to follow up with sample coverage. If you throw enough of your exceptional samples against that wall, something is likely to stick.

All of the aforementioned methods take the direct, through-the-front-door approach. But in an effort to reach one of these companies, it is equally important for you just to talk to everyone you know about your pursuit of reading work. Certainly, if you know an assistant, story editor, creative executive, or director of development, talk to them and nurture those relationships. These are the people who are hiring readers on behalf of the major companies. If they're not hiring, they will probably know someone who is.

If, however, you are not acquainted with any of these professionals, talk and talk and talk to *everyone else on the planet*. I assure you, everyone is somehow connected to somebody who is somehow working in the entertainment industry. If you talk it up enough, a referral is bound to surface here and there. It may not necessarily be a studio or agency referral, but realize that anyone in any way associated with the film/TV industry has probably wanted feedback on one of their own creative projects or wanted someone else to read a script, book, treatment, play, or comic book so they don't have to. I'm talking anyone. I worked as a grip once, and I can tell you that the grips are writing screenplays as much as everyone else in the business. So are props people and special effects techs, and painters, editors, cameramen, and sound guys. As I write this, I am expecting a script in from a stunt man. Perhaps one of these people will agree to pay you for your honest, experienced feedback.

Also know that screenplay contests abound these days. Everyone from local film offices to curious private investors is putting out a call for entries for "the next great screenwriting competition." Many will need at least a reader or two to sort through the stack of submissions they will inevitably receive from the latest crop of starving, hopeful writers. Some will tell you that they're having volunteers and/or certain amateurs take care of their reading for them. If there is room for some sales chat, *convince them* that a volunteer won't examine their submissions with the professionalism, experience, and quick turnaround that you would for nominal pay.

In addition to contests, there are also coverage services out there—such as my own Readers Unlimited—that hire new readers from time to time. These companies provide experienced, professional story analysis to producers, directors, writers, and others. Sometimes, such coverage services are the ones that sort through the initial round of submissions for a screenplay contest. While the ratio of résumés received to available work is usually quite uneven, many coverage companies do like to maintain a "deep bench" in the event of an unexpected surge of submissions or the sudden unavailability of one of their regular analysts.

Although, it is not just within the "connected" sector where your next client may be hiding. I remember setting up online banking for my company, and the service rep who was helping me on the phone asked me about what I do. After giving him a twenty-second spiel about my coverage service, I learned that this gentleman was up in Northern California and had four screenplays on which he desperately wanted professional feedback but didn't know where to turn. As a result of my "tell the world about it" policy, I found myself with a new client from an unexpected place. Maybe it's your attorney, accountant, plumber, cab driver, or ex-boyfriend who will surface as that first paying customer to set you on your way as a professional reader.

No matter who the targeted client is, follow up will become important. Rarely can one walk through a company's door or ask an individual for reading work and land herself an immediate gig. Remember, one prospective client might have hundreds of scripts to process a month; another client might be hesitant to shell out the cash; another might have other readers in mind; another might be rewriting and rewriting. In none of these cases will their first thought be you. Those first few, especially, will require persistence, perhaps an emphasis on some personal connection, and whatever other sales techniques you can employ to seal the deal.

And If That Doesn't Work . . .

Then again, there are no guarantees. It might happen that you've talked it up till you're blue in the face, but to no avail, and you are still desperate to tag those first few scripts onto your résumé. As you tell the world about your endeavors, you might try going a step further by offering to intern for a company or individual. To many outfits, intern signifies "feast of free labor," and they will bite. If you can arrange to serve as a reading intern alone, all the better. With that company, establish in advance how many scripts per week you would be willing to look at for no charge.

Usually, though, interning will require you to make an appearance at an office to help out with some administrative duties. If you're starting out in the business and have the time and finances to get you through a day or two a week, I highly recommend it. Just make sure that reading duties come with the internship, and after you get your feet wet, advocate for sitting in on company story/development meetings, where you might be asked to verbalize your thoughts on certain scripts. Keep your ears and eyes open and the experience will prove invaluable. And in all likelihood, your hard work will turn into some pay for your reading and/or administrative services. On a number of occasions, I have seen development interns go on to become full-time readers or assistants and continue on up the ranks. Some of them are running major companies now, and it all started with their offering to read a script or two for free.

As a variation of the internship, there is also pro bono work, which you could offer to struggling writers, directors, actors, producers, and so on, who cannot afford to pay much or anything at all. There are plenty of them out there. Worst-case scenario: you will walk away with more practice, a few more samples for your portfolio, and another addition to your résumé. Best-case scenario: you will generate positive word-of-mouth or referrals to paying clients. *Do not, however, allow your pro bono services to go too far. Many will try to take advantage of your gracious offer.* One or two scripts for a few different people, sure. Anything more than that, and it starts to become a waste of your energy. With no pay to show for your efforts, you are apt to burn out quickly. While reading pro bono, let these fortunate freeloaders know that reading scripts is typically what you do for a living. Don't be afraid to ask them to send clients your way.

Spec Coverage

While applying for reading work, in addition to your own samples, a company may ask you to write spec coverage. As a screenwriter may pen a script "on spec" (i.e., write for free with speculation as to whether it ever will be optioned or purchased), it is, in this case, speculation as to whether you will be hired as a reader. Simply stated, it is a tryout. The prospective client will probably give you a couple of scripts that they know—in order to gauge your tastes and ideas versus theirs—and then ask you to return coverage to them within a short amount of time. If they like what they see, perhaps it will lead to some work for their company. If not, you walk away with the practice and a couple more samples for your portfolio.

Unless you're eager for real work simulation or to make an extreme impression somewhere, do not offer to write spec coverage for a company—let them ask you for it. Try not to write spec coverage for every company that asks, either. This is a good way to lose faith in the practice of script reading altogether. If it is an entity for whom you desperately want to work and you are convinced that you have a strong shot at being hired, then go for it. But it might not be worth the hassle and heartbreak to do spec coverage for companies that will only promise to keep your samples on file or for smaller companies that aren't guaranteed to offer much work even if and when they do bring you on.

Must I Live on a "Coast"?

Were I writing this ten years ago, I would have told you that it is extremely important to live in New York, Los Angeles, or London to maintain consistent script analysis work. Back then, the most common modus operandi for script distribution was to have story analysts come into an office to pick up scripts and then return them with completed coverage clipped on top. For those lucky few, a wealthy company might have couriered the work to a reader's home/office. To mail scripts to readers elsewhere in the country didn't make sense, in light of the cost and time and a host of other experienced readers on call in town. Okay, I did have one friend who, in the mid-nineties, was living in Los Angeles but received scripts from Miramax in New York via Fed Ex on a weekly basis. Still, that was a bicoastal situation.

The practice of distributing printed scripts in New York and L.A. is still in existence, but, thanks to technology, I would label that "so twentieth century." It is becoming increasingly possible to offer your story analysis services elsewhere. First, everyone is e-mailing scripts to everyone else nowadays; e-mailing scripts and coverage has achieved the norm in the practice of story analysis. It is easier, faster, and cheaper for everyone. So, if you can land a client in Los Angeles, he can e-mail you the reading material just as easily as—if not more easily than—having someone come to pick up a hard copy. And the moment you finish your work, you can return the evaluation to your client instantaneously by hitting send, just the same as anyone locally. At my company in Los Angeles, I have hired readers from Mexico to San Francisco to South Africa.

Also beneficial to those hoping to avoid residence within an urban entertainment hub is the rise of digital technology. Today, it is relatively cheap to grab a DV camera and a computer editing system such as Pro Tools and make one's own independent film on one's own turf. Suddenly, the film business isn't just for the mega-bankrolls of the studio system. It is also possible for the "everyman" to set up shop as an indie producer anywhere in the country or the world. Hence, in your own backyard you might be able to tap into two or three of these producers and develop a bit of a niche for yourself.

It's not just technology, however, that has surged. In any city you visit, you will find a growing general awareness for film development and production. Perhaps with the aid of the Internet, people have been able to learn and track more about the writing, development, production, and distribution processes. Suddenly, they're talking about weekend grosses in the Heartland. Tax incentives, too, are proving to be a draw to filmmakers in states such as New Mexico and Louisiana. This burgeoning grassroots enthusiasm can only feed local film communities with money and material, not to mention new writers, directors, producers, and facilities—all of whom are going to want objective, honest feedback on their projects from someone who has already read a number of scripts with a critical eye.

Naturally, the tough part is getting those first few paying clients. If steady reading work is what you are pursuing, realistically, it may behoove you to start your career on a "coast" or in some other mini-hub such as Chicago, Vancouver, Toronto, or Austin. Or you might have to—at the very least—visit there often to get yourself started. After you have accumulated some experience points, however, there is not much these days to prevent you from living anywhere and securing some degree of workflow. For all intents and purposes, as long as you have Internet access, you can live in the Himalayas and work as a story analyst. All it takes is that one first script, which could easily turn into a few, if not tens, if not hundreds.

10

Once You Do Get Work

Congratulations! So, you have read a script or two and have been compensated and you are now a full-fledged story analyst. Now what happens? If at this point you have not decided that it's a rotten line of work and you would like to continue to be compensated for your script coverage, then it is time to set your mind on nurturing relationships with the clients you have and finding new ones. But before turning your attention to those items, it is important that you know a few things about the life of a professional story analyst—all of which will either entice you further or scare you away forever.

The Life (and Pay) of a Reader

The life of the professional script reader is much like that of many other independent contractors. So is the pay—that is, variable in amount and frequency. Most story analysts are compensated for basic coverage with something between $25 and $90 per script. Factors that could affect this amount may include the type of coverage you are asked to write, the length of the coverage, the length of the reading material, the turnaround time, and your client's wealth and generosity (or lack thereof). If asked to write standard full coverage—including a top sheet, one to two pages of synopsis, and one to two pages of commentary within forty-eight hours for a script under 135 pages—it would be reasonable to expect a *bare minimum* of $40 per script. Asked to write coverage overnight? To cover a script over 135 pages? To write a lengthy synopsis and/or comments with character breakdown? To add detailed rewrite suggestions? It wouldn't be out of the question for you to request more than standard pay.

There are also factors that affect frequency of story analysis work. For instance, when I was reading full time, I came to realize that the slow periods arrived just before and during major holidays and film festivals, when seemingly the entire industry pours out of town for other lands. I also knew to expect a tidal wave of work within a week of my clients' return from these calendar events. Whether away for work or for play, they would usually arrive home with a stack of scripts under their arm and another one or two piles awaiting them on their desk. Other times, however, there are simply inexplicable lulls and peaks in the workload. I have found that the work volume is sort of like the stock market—extremely sensitive to world events, strike fears, weather conditions, special announcements, breaking news, and the latest traffic snarl.

Given the above considerations, it is extremely difficult to offer you an estimated annual figure, assuming standard story analysis is indeed your sole source of income. Let's say, however, you're in a groove with a few regular clients and doing a fine job; I will go so far as to supply a ballpark range. On the low end, you might receive three or four a week at $55 per script, which would only come to about $10,000 annually. On the other end, I've seen some story analysts pore through an average of ten scripts weekly for $75 apiece or more and pull in about $35,000 per year.

By entry-level standards the above totals are about average. If, however, you go by other standards, you might have a problem with these figures. Do know that reading work can be quite sporadic. One can have terrific years and dismal years, as is the case with any area of consulting. You *can* make a living at it, full-time—especially if you begin to branch out with the type of services you offer (see the "Taking It to the Next Level" segment in this chapter). I have one friend who, for a spell, supported a wife and twin children as a professional story analyst while maintaining a respectable quality of life. But the next question would be, do you *want* to make a living at it? Before answering that, examine a few more pros and cons:

Cons

1. I have often jested that the life of a story analyst can mirror that of a professional assassin: you spend your days lying low in a shadowy place, waiting for the phone to ring. And then you get the call—they want you to "kill somebody's baby." A brief surge of excitement, and then it's back to waiting for the phone to ring again with that next assignment. I say "kill" because, as emphasized earlier, 90 to 95 percent of the material you read will warrant a Pass recommendation, often signifying the end of the line for that particular work on your client's radar. I say "baby" because the material will have been conceived and born only after hours of labor by one or more writers who—in all likelihood—will look upon their work with great love. It can be a grisly existence.

2. Imagine reading mostly bad books from cover to cover, day-in/day-out, and then having to explain all the reasons why you think they're so poor. Remember, you usually won't have the luxury of putting it down if you don't like it; you'll have to synopsize and comment on it accurately from start to finish. It can be draining. And at the end of the day, since you spent your entire day looking at words, the last thing on earth you will want to do is sit down with a good book or look at a newspaper. I can't remember the last time I did any significant amount of pleasure reading.

3. Most readers do their work from home. There's little office culture available. Water cooler talk amounts to the occasional grunt to your goldfish about being overworked and underpaid.

Office potluck means whatever condiments you can find rotting in your fridge. That also means that there's little to no positive feedback. Your client will be too busy to think of giving out "reader-of-the-month" awards or e-mail you with that occasional pat on the back.

4. You will be working on constant deadlines. Just when you get one report into your client's inbox, the next job could come at you. While you might be grateful to have the work, there could always be something hanging over your head.

5. The Tax Man takes a lot out of the pockets of a self-employed contractor—anywhere between 25 and 45 percent, counting federal and state taxes. You will likely have to file quarterly estimated payments with what could seem to be hefty checks. Also know that self-employed independent contractors are sometimes placed prominently on the IRS radar. Before beginning this lifestyle, make sure you have a conversation with your own accountant or attorney. (Self-employed consultant status only applies if you receive 1099 forms from the companies you are reading for. If you receive W-2s, you are classified as an employee.)

6. No benefits: no health plan, no dental or vision, no sick days or vacation days or personal days to accrue, no equity in a business, no overtime, no expense account, no bonuses, and you won't be paying into any corporate retirement plan or social security. You will often have to work nights and weekends to meet your deadlines.

Pros

1. Maybe the life of an "assassin" is just the thing for you. After all, you are practically your own boss. While at first it might be work when you can get it, it could turn into work when you *want* it. You are the Specialist, the go-to guy, the

one they call in to do their dirty work. I've seen some take pride in this weighted and unique responsibility. Dare I suggest that some out there relish dissecting and obliterating poor writing?

2. Working from home can itself be a significant benefit. Every day is casual Friday to the extreme. You can freely check personal e-mail and Web sites without Big Brother watching from some Master Server. The commute may only be a few paces from bed to your home office armoire, which means no gas expenses or vehicle wear and tear. Sure, there's a small chance you may be required to pick up scripts from your client, but even then, there will probably be some flexibility for the pick-up time, allowing you to avoid rush-hour traffic. Need a power nap? Want to run a quick errand or two in the middle of the day? Go ahead!

3. The Tax Man taketh away, but remember he also giveth write-offs. Again, I urge you to discuss this issue with your accountant or attorney, but you can realistically anticipate that e-mail and phone service and a few monthly meals for business/client development will amount to a tax break. Moreover, since you are a consultant in the entertainment world, all related magazine, movie, DVD, Internet, and television purchases, rentals, or services could technically qualify as write-offs in the category of research. Music purchases, too, may occasionally qualify. According to Mitchell Miller, Beverly Hills entertainment tax attorney, "The key here is to document everything. What project the DVD rental was related to, whom you took to lunch and what you discussed—document every expense. I also advise clients not to claim a portion of your housing, a portion of your utilities, etc., as deductions. Doing that is waving a flag in front of the IRS that says, 'Audit me, audit me!' The few extra bucks of tax reduction won't make up for the pain and aggravation."

4. Especially in your first few years of reading for a living, your learning curve will ascend steeply. In fact, story analysis is great preparation for what you might see as your next career step. Writers, directors, producers, and development executives must all know story: how to discuss it, how to dissect it, how to rework it. By reading volumes of scripts as a professional, you will undoubtedly acquire these skills yourself.

So, when all is said and done, the life of a professional story analyst is the life of any independent contractor. I'm not going to encourage it or discourage it. You know who you are and the nature of your needs, desires, schedule, and capabilities. Assuming your commitment, however, you will next want to put your mind toward maintaining the workload.

Five Ways to Keep Your Client Satisfied

Remember how I mentioned that there's no positive feedback? Allow me to qualify the statement: there is positive feedback, but it usually comes in the form of *silence*. If your client hasn't said a thing to you in months other than, "Thanks, here's another one," then assume you're doing a great job. On the other hand, chances are you will be hearing from your client if you violate a few tacit rules. Adhere to the following checklist to ensure yourself plenty of silence:

1. *Never, never, never miss a deadline.* No matter who the client is, they would not have gotten the property covered if they weren't hungry for an opinion on it. If you agree on a certain time and then disappoint them by turning your report in a day or an hour or even twenty minutes late, you could easily brand yourself as unreliable to them and everyone within their network. Speaking as one who runs a coverage service, I give work first to those readers who habitually turn in their coverage early. There is too much else going on in people's daily routines to worry about whether the coverage will be there on time.

2. *Report accurately in your synopsis.* That may seem like a no-brainer to you, but with deadlines and poor writing and other scripts and activities and distractions awaiting them, readers are apt to scribble inaccurate synopses as they hurry through material. And it can get them in trouble. Pretend you're reading for a development executive who then uses your coverage as a basis for rejecting a certain producer's project. The exec backs up his argument with those thoughts outlined in your comments, but the exec and producer are friendly enough that your client agrees to e-mail the producer the coverage to further support the official "Pasadena." This does happen on occasion. The producer will inevitably look through your synopsis along with the comments. He might even show it to his staff and, possibly, the writer. If there is an error or two in your synopsis, somebody is bound to notice them. Then the producer calls up your client, whining, angry that your reader doesn't know what she's talking about because x and y never happen that way in the story. He might even insist that your client read or re-read the script, making it generally uncomfortable for him, and the discomfort will ultimately rain down on you. You just never know in whose hands your coverage will land.

Moreover, no matter how poor the material, there is something unjust about characterizing a story differently than it has actually been written. Certainly, synopsize as efficiently as you can. You will inevitably have to disregard certain events and characters to summarize the property within a couple of pages. The concept of selective omission, however, is not the same as describing events that never actually transpire. Be careful not to sacrifice accuracy for speed.

3. *Keep your comments consistent with the recommendation and other top sheet items.* There is nothing more dizzying for a client than reading coverage that says "yes" on one page

and "no" on the next. You've been hired because your client wants a concrete suggestion: don't waste your time, make this movie tomorrow, or read the script when you can because there's something about this one. Create a stance and stick to it. While you should feel free to add a hint of praise or encouragement in your comments for a "Pass" project, don't offer a laundry list of virtues. If your comment summary declares that a script has a strong premise, well-developed characters, yet a poor plot, make sure that you go on to support each of those with examples, rather than expanding only on, say, structure, tone shift, and theme.

4. *Respect client confidentiality.* If you're a professional story analyst, chances are you won't be able to make a living reading for one client alone. Your client can't expect you to read solely for them, either, unless the deal is just that good. They will, however, require you to keep confidential all matters and material specific to their operation. The reasons for confidentiality can vary. Perhaps an agent or writer sneaks your client a script in advance of "going wide" with it (i.e., submitting it to several parties simultaneously). If you start telling others about this wonderful script you've covered from such and such, you might sacrifice your client's pre-arranged edge over the rest of the market. On the other hand, you could summarily tarnish both the client's relationship with the submitter and the submitter's own reputation if you openly babble about this awful script you've come across. Maybe your client has told the submitter that they would read it themselves, when actually you're doing the reading for them. Or you might end up reading for someone who is test marketing their project with you, and they would rather their hot new premise not be leaked to potential competitors.

There were times when I was reading that I would receive the same script from two different clients within weeks or even days of each other. This happens, usually when agents and managers go wide with a property. First of all, it's good work if you can get it, seeing how you'll be getting paid two for one. Therefore, it does not benefit anyone if you tell your client that you've seen this before or that you're in the process of covering it for someone else. Just quietly thank them for the work and cut and paste away into their template.

In short, absolutely pursue multiple clients, but try to keep it zipped from job to job. Loose lips can sink your ship.

5. *Make the right recommendation and be sure you mean it.* Oh, the bells and whistles that sound in an office when "Recommend" coverage comes in. The client will say to himself, "This is it. This is the project I've been waiting for all these years. The one that's going to win me that Oscar, pay me those millions, label me a made guy." Dampening the pages with eager drool, he begins the script: Page 1, "Okay, interesting, but I'm not completely hooked yet" . . . Page 5, "Okay, but where are the fireworks?" . . . Page 11, "What is this crap?!?" . . . Page 23, *"This reader must die!!"*

Imagine the disappointment if you labeled something "Recommend" that your client would clearly call "Poor." It could generate some unwanted animosity. I have personally had to "discontinue" a reader for submitting gushingly favorable coverage when my employer thought the project was particularly horrible. I can't say I disagreed with the employer, either. Still, the issue wasn't so much that the reader gave a "Recommend" to not-so-great material as it was that the reader couldn't adequately defend his conclusion. Usually when you stamp a property with that rare "Recommend," it says to the client that *you're willing to stake your career and reputation on this one*, and if you had the money, you would produce this project yourself without hesitation. It screams, "Drop everything and read this now!" and the client will undoubtedly follow that suggestion.

On the flip side, the question always comes up, "What if I pass on something that goes on to make millions and win awards?" Most readers have done it, as have many executives. Often you will read earlier drafts of scripts that are far from stellar, no matter how you slice it, and in the end there's no shame in having said that this particular draft is rather poor or without commercial potential.

Okay, here's my own story:

Five years before it was produced, I read a draft of the manuscript (i.e., the book version) for *Sideways* for Paramount Classics (now Paramount Vantage). I recommended a "Pass." Sure, I could have told you that if an exceptional director such as Alexander Payne came onboard and worked on it for four more years, it would have great potential. That's implicit for any poorly written script—anything's fixable if you're willing to invest the right amount of toil and expense. I, however, was covering what was given to me—the book (or a draft of it) on which Alexander Payne and Jim Taylor eventually based their screenplay. The manuscript I read included, among other things: encounters with a rifle-toting boar hunter; a private investigator who blackmails Jack (eventually played by Thomas Haden Church), leaving Miles (eventually played by Paul Giamatti) to return to his mother's house to steal from her safe; various other run-ins with conservative tourists and residents (like the one on the golf course in the film version); and a more together, less nebbish main character. I wrote in my coverage that the shenanigans get old, the characters are never that likeable, it was openly derivative of one of my favorite films (*Withnail & I*), and that the story was a male fantasy geared mostly toward white, older, educated men (i.e., not an historically lucrative market). The point is, I made that (and every) recommendation with confidence, knowing I had the ammo with which to back up my opinion if anyone came after me for it.

I don't know if Paramount passed on *Sideways* strictly based on my recommendation, but when it happens that one of your Passes goes on to perform well elsewhere, a sickening *mea culpa* does wash over you. Still, if you can clearly support your recommendation, you can rest easy that you've done the best any reader can do with what you were given. And if they actually end up reading and loving material that you recommend against? Well, a bit of psychology could come into play. The pleasant surprise at having found something they like will probably mitigate any disparaging thoughts toward the reader who wrote "Pass" on the coverage. Not only that, but in an industry of total insecurity, a client might be inclined to heed your criticism and tone down the enthusiasm a notch, even if instincts are telling them that the material is wonderful. If this critic (you, the reader, that is) didn't like it, then maybe there will be others, too? These thoughts will probably consume them before those about shooting the messenger.

None of this is to say you should balk at handing out a recommendation. If you truly believe the property warrants a "Recommend" or a "Pass," then by all means give it that recommendation. Trust your own instincts, but be well prepared to discuss verbally and in writing how the material succeeds or fails, element by element. Be able to support your opinion, as if it were fact.

The Issue of Subjectivity

Yes, the problem is we all know that the art and business of screenplay story analysis involves very little fact. It's an altogether subjective practice—or is it?

You should know that the above case of one person's trash being another's treasure is an extreme example. I like to think there is *some degree* of science (yes, science) to the practice of story analysis deriving from my own Twin Theories of the Happy Medium:

> *A relatively well-written script, in its present form, is bound to fall somewhere between decent and excellent in the eyes of a vast majority of experienced readers.*

and

> *A relatively flawed script, in its present form, is bound to fall somewhere between dreadful and decent in the eyes of a vast majority of experienced readers.*

I have tested these theories in story analysis workshops, and they work.

By these standards, chances are that you will not lose your gig with a client if you call it a "Recommend." If you really enjoyed it that much, there is probably enough there for anyone to enjoy to some extent. Perhaps the client would not have given it a "Recommend" but a "Consider" or even a "Weak Consider." At that point, the client would probably acknowledge that coverage isn't science, understand your well-supported point, agree to disagree, and move on. Conversely, if you stamp a script with a "Pass," chances are that your employer will not go to the other extreme and digest it as one of his top ten favorites. They might go as high as a "Consider" in their mind but they will inevitably see your point and get on with it.

There are other factors associated with subjectivity that come into play when reading scripts. Rest assured that each item below will enter your mind and/or ears as you declare yourself a professional story analyst.

"Readers Are Paid to Pass on Scripts"

I've heard many say this about the practice of story analysis, but don't let this fallacy get under your skin. People who express this sentiment are quite often frustrated writers or producers who have received consistently poor coverage on their own projects. Like producers and executives, you will unavoidably go into every script *wanting* to *love* that script. You will soon realize that it is more of a drain, psychologically and time wise, to cover the underperforming script, whereas you will find it surprisingly invigorating to evaluate strong material. Who doesn't like to sit down to the equivalent of a good book or an entertaining movie and then share the enthusiasm?

Also, there is some degree of reward to be had for pointing out great material, if only the personal satisfaction of seeing something you liked make it to the screen. It has been personally gratifying to have assigned a Consider or Recommend to projects that have, at the very least, conquered the odds and been produced (even if some were made by a company other than the client for whom I read), including: *The Truman Show, Assassins, Ghost Dog, The Luzhin Defense, Donnie Brasco, Dangerous Minds, Henry Fool, Sling Blade, The Snow Walker, Marvin's Room, The English Patient, Memento, The Illusionist,* and *Artie Lange's Beer League.* Your encounter with a strong property could also mean good fortune for your client, which in turn could trickle down to you in the form of more work, advancement within the company, and/or general goodwill for being the bearer of terrific news. It would also be acceptable to list successful and produced films that you have recommended on your résumé.

True, you may be asked to enter your reading with a hypercritical eye, but this mandate won't predispose you to abhor the property. You will still *want* to *love* it, not to pass on it.

"Who Are You to Judge Me?" (a.k.a. "Who Am I to Judge You?")

On occasion I've been asked the first question above by disgruntled clients whose scripts I critiqued unfavorably. Many other times, in fits of insecurity, I've asked the myself the second question. Now, statistics probably do support the notion that the majority of readers are writers who have been bashed by other readers. Even so, that's not who readers *are*. Rest assured, I have seen many, many story analysts become so knowledgeable from their years of reading hundreds of scripts that they do, in fact, go on to become paid feature or TV writers, directors, producers, and executives. For example, I remember hiring Matt Alvarez as a development intern; he now runs Ice Cube's company, Cube Vision. Refer to producer Craig Perry's foreword in this book for another example of someone who started as a script reader and went on to do great things. Many others I know have already made money as writers, producers, directors, or execs but are in need of extra cash until that next gig comes in. And sometimes a company will hire an intern right out of college specifically for her fresh, youthful outlook on material. These individuals might reside within the target audience of the company's mandate and, in that case, the company will consider that intern to be the perfect person to judge.

Regardless of the objections to it, story analysis is a practice that has changed very little over the years. Companies and other clients find readers whose opinions they respect and trust, and they stick with them. Their readers are people whose opinions coincide with their own the majority of the time. Again, it comes down to William Goldman's "Nobody knows anything." You don't have to be Steven Spielberg or Roger Ebert to intelligently and honestly express why you like or dislike a property. Those folks have made as many—if not more—mistakes as you ever will. You don't even necessarily have to have worked as a production assistant or development intern. So who are you to judge, then? I bet you are someone with a brain, an opinion, a strong understanding of screenwriting fundamentals, the ability to communicate an argument with supporting examples, a passion for filmed entertainment, and a computer. And that's what is required. (Granted, if even one of those doesn't apply to you, then either do something to change that or don't get into script reading.)

In the end, the more scripts you read and the more years you do it, the less you will be questioned about who you are.

"I'm Having a Bad Day"

It's an obvious concern about the coverage system: What if that one person who can yea or nay a script simply wakes up on the wrong side of the bed? It will happen to you. The dog will defecate on the floor or your three-year-old daughter will tell you she hates you or a check will bounce or your football team will have lost in the playoffs. That's life, and no matter the field, that's the baggage people bring to work with them each day. But you do have a job to do and a duty to be fair and objective in the critiques you offer. It becomes an obvious lesson in psychology.

Before reading that script, of course, do your best to distance yourself from those elements that are "poisoning" your mood. Create a buffer. Watch some TV (though daytime TV could just as easily push you over the edge). Go for a quick walk. Vent to someone. Eat some chocolate, even if it is only 7 A.M. If you go into the job hating the universe, then chances are that material is going to feel your wrath, which is really unfair to your client and to yourself. Think of it this way: most people go into a movie in a good mood, in anticipation of some fun, engaging, or meaningful entertainment or drama. If you can't at that moment enter the work in that mindset, then take a breather.

On the other hand, you may not always have the luxury of putting off the work until you're feeling more chipper. After all, coverage is a service usually performed on a tight deadline. Even so, on the "bad day" factor, I have told concerned clients that much as a good film can transform a viewer's frame of mind, so will a great script handily circumvent a reader's sour state. Regardless of mood, an experienced professional who is well versed in the fundamentals of screenwriting will fall within the guidelines of those Twin Theories of the Happy Medium. The seasoned pro will have evaluated enough scripts to be able to discern poor from strong material, and that poorly written material will garner somewhere between an intensely negative to a lukewarm reaction and a solidly written property will generate lukewarm to gushingly positive feedback.

Five Responses to the Disgruntled Client

Of course, the above thoughts on subjectivity imply that you *will* come across the occasional individual who, in some way, will question your ability to judge their material. Screenwriting and filmmaking, like any art, can be a very passionate and personal aspect of your clients' lives, especially if they are writers, producers, or directors who have invested loads of time and money into the project. Then, here you come along and—in the matter of a few hours—dismiss their work as a "Pass," heaping it with 95 percent of the other scripts you've read. Even if you have been extremely diplomatic and constructive in your evaluation, there are many out there who are unprepared to accept what you have to tell them.

Before taking on work, it will be up to you to assess the mindset of each client. Most walk into coverage eager for tips on how to improve their material. But I have had writers and producers come to me for coverage, convinced that theirs is a final draft destined to make them millions in the market tomorrow, only to be handed a deserved "Pass" recommendation. If this type of client falls into your radar, it's important that you offer a verbal disclaimer—that yours is only one opinion and that they must be prepared for an objective, constructive critique of their property. Despite such a disclaimer, some still might only hear what they want to hear. If you view the material any differently than how they intended you to view it, reactions can range from slightly miffed to wholly indignant to furious. If they keep it to themselves for the most part, just let it go. Chances are, within the next few weeks, they will study and study your coverage, match it up with their work, and begin to understand your perspective. At this point, they might even complete a rewrite and send it back to you for repeat business. (I have had clients who were initially peeved send their scripts back to me six times or more in an attempt to get it right.)

If, however, it becomes a situation in which someone questions your character and/or ability, you should be prepared to respond with logic and diplomacy, if only for the sake of your own reputation and dignity. The following five responses may seem unduly negative or paranoid to you, but they do stem from the harsh reality of the business. I have unfortunately been in situations where I've had to use each of these. I invite you to pocket any or all of them, just in case:

1. "Unfortunately, professional readers aren't paid to tell people what they want to hear. Good readers pick out the major flaws in a script and point the material in the right direction." Okay, there is that rare occasion where you will be asked to create some political coverage, but they don't need to know that. Overwhelmingly so, your duty will be to provide a great degree of truth as to how you feel about the material.

2. "As a writer and artist, you assume the risk that people are going to critique your work, and not always favorably so."

3. "While you may not agree with my argument, I have supported it clearly with specific examples and constructive rewrite suggestions." Again, make sure that this fact does, indeed, apply to your coverage.

4. "You're not alone. About 95 percent of all scripts that are read professionally receive a 'Pass' grade. That's not to say I wanted to give this a 'Pass,' but today's standards and finite resources make it that difficult to receive anything more on a

script." If the script is a first draft, that's extra ammo for you in this category. You could say, "Hey, it's called a first draft for a reason." You might go on to encourage them to try a rewrite and see what happens.

5. And then there's the one you might use once or twice in ten thousand for the uncomfortably rabid client whose business you can take or leave after the insults have flown. If you are confident enough with your own take on the script, as you should be, and the situation really warrants it, you could resort to this: "If you truly think my judgment is that invalid, I invite you to visit one or more of my well-established competitors. If the feedback you receive from any of them on this particular draft is significantly more favorable than mine (i.e., if you receive a 'Strong Consider' or 'Recommend' on the work), I will happily reimburse you for both their services and mine." On the *one* occasion when it did get to this point for me, I went so far as to provide links to Web sites and e-mail addresses for other readers and coverage services. The client saw how much I believed in my work, and the discussion never went any further.

Allow me to emphasize that none of the above five responses should be spouted liberally. Though they should be expressed with confidence and conviction, think of them more as a last resort. And if those don't soothe your client—if they are that disgruntled—I urge you to just let it go, because after a while you could burn out, you could damage your reputation, and it can become a case of throwing good money after bad.

Increasing Your Work Load

In addition to keeping your current clients happy, you will begin to think about attracting new ones (assuming you haven't started up as a full-time studio reader with a guaranteed, constant workflow from one source). Whatever worked enough for you to nab your first few clients, certainly keep at it for the fourth, fifth, sixth, tenth, and so on; continue to nurture that portfolio and get it out there, hit the job lists, send more queries, do the occasional free-bie, and talk to *everyone on Earth* about your career. Still there are additional paths you might consider in the interest of widen-ing your net. Many busy story analysts are now posting their own Web sites, which include personal and professional information, samples of their work, a list of clients past and present, and what-ever content they may be able to dream up. Similarly, a periodic e-mail newsletter might help remind prospects that you're still there and that your experienced, objective opinion is still on call for them.

Film festivals and film schools all over the world often host industry professionals to sit on panels or make presentations about their experiences and knowledge. The more you read professionally, the more you can confidently call yourself a sea-soned entertainment professional. Try contacting these festivals and schools and offer your wisdom for such panels, workshops, and lectures. If invited, don't forget your business card.

Put your friends and clients to work for you as your personal sales team. Offer them discounts, bonuses, or other incentives for referrals. Even the closest friend might not remember to put a word in for you with a prospect, but the promise of a dinner out or a bottle of something will show them how much it means to you and could give them enough push to help you land that one client that keeps you busy for months. Currently, the bulk of my business is referral-based.

Flexibility, too, might grab the otherwise hesitant or unin-terested prospect. Imagine you are sitting on an airplane next to a stranger, you start making small talk, and it eventually comes out what you do for a living. He tells you he's actually an independent producer and, in a perfect world, would love to be able to use your services. He has this stack of ten submissions sitting on his desk, and he can't seem to get to any of them.

He goes on to ask you your rate. When you tell him it's $75 per script on standard coverage, he replies that this is the problem: he doesn't want to (or can't afford to) pay an experienced analyst reading fees like that for so many scripts. So, you offer to budge a little on your standard rate and read them in "bulk" for $65 each. After all, $650 from this client would be better than $0, right? He continues to shrug it off; he'll just get to them himself when he can. So then you present him with two options:

Option A: You will read a few of the scripts, perhaps the more promising ones, to at least take the edge off that growing mound. If he bites, it would, of course, give you the opportunity to show off your talents and hook him for future work.

Option B: You can reduce the fee on each script by reducing the length of your synopsis and/or comments (e.g., down to a half page from your usual one to two pages). The coverage may not be as comprehensive, but he would still be receiving a solid overview and objective opinion to help him prioritize his reading schedule. If the $45 (or so) per script you propose for this reduced service is still too rich for his blood, you could go on to propose a cover page alone at even a lower rate. This service would at least provide him with a general but reliable impression of each script before deciding which to read first (or at all).

In sum, if you are not dealing with a prospect such as a studio or agency that only works with a fixed template, offer to flex your standard coverage to meet the needs of a prospective client, though don't sell yourself short. Make sure the income per script sufficiently compensates you for the amount of time and effort you will have to put into that report.

Again, the life of a freelance story analyst is much like that of an independent consultant in any industry, and to go on would mean to write an entire new book on the practice of consulting itself. But those books have been written already, and I recommend you pick up one or two if you aim to establish yourself as a professional reader. One I came across as I began my coverage firm was *Getting Started in Consulting*, by Alan Weiss, Ph.D. (John Wiley & Sons, Inc.), an easy read that provides pertinent pointers on topics such as advanced techniques for marketing yourself and a relevant "Forty Ways to Increase Your Fees."

Taking It to the Next Level

For many, story analysis will serve as supplemental income—that change of pace or extra cash in your pocket while you work that nine to fiver. For a few, freelance story analysis will become a career. I have made a living at it for years, and I know some who have been doing it full time for longer than I have. For those who are extremely serious about becoming a career reader, you might attempt to hook up with the Story Analyst Union in Los Angeles, which services the major studios. If you're able to secure a nomination into this exclusive (and elusive) bunch—currently merged with the Editors Guild—it could turn into a salaried position in your own trailer on a studio lot, for which you will read about two scripts per day, five days a week. Among other things, you will have to rack up some experience points and do some fancy networking before you can achieve union status.

For the majority who enter the world of coverage, however, it is viewed as a stepping-stone into various other opportunities within the entertainment industry. One logical step up from standard coverage is the practice of development notes, also called story notes. Depending on the client's specs, notes may or may not require a cover page and synopsis. Regardless, the heart of development notes is the comments section, which goes into far more detail than coverage and picks apart a script element by element. Such a report will usually total between five and ten pages. Though notes will require more time, effort, and insight on your part, in some ways, notes can be easier than coverage. With coverage, you are usually allocated two pages, maximum, for your comments, while you may feel you could actually pen a dissertation about why something works or doesn't. Development notes, however, give you the leeway to flesh out your opinion with extra examples and recommendations and rarely come with a ceiling on the page count. With notes, however, you think not only critically but creatively, as a solid report will also provide rewrite suggestions. In this case, you will have to become the writer's partner for a moment. You will have to make revision recommendations to reflect what you would like to see happen differently in the script or what the market demands are for such a story.

Some story analysts notes will even conclude with "Page Notes," which direct a client to specific page numbers or script sections and, in one to three sentences, point out anything from typos to awkward dialogue to more examples to support your comments. Naturally, the added work that you put into development notes should also amount to extra pay. Rates for a standard notes job can range from $80 to $500. Not everyone will approach it in the same way, but in Appendix F you will find the guidelines for development notes that I hand to my readers. As this type of work requires an advanced, extensive critique, I do not recommend pursuing it until you feel you have firmly and expertly grasped the practice of story analysis and advanced screenwriting technique.

Some also offer clients phone consults that might be viewed as the verbal version of development notes. For the client, notes and phone consults each have advantages and disadvantages. With development notes, clients receive a hard copy (and/or e-mail) of the report, which they will have in front of them to reflect on as much as they like as they embark on their rewrite process. But there is a sort of finality to notes—what you get is what you get. The angles you critique or recommend may not be everything the client wanted or needed to know.

Phone consultation, on the other hand, provides a more interactive avenue, like a one-on-one with a screenwriting tutor for a specified amount of time. It gives you, the consultant, the chance to ask the client questions (e.g., What was your intention with this character? This scene? Your theme?) and react/adjust thoughts accordingly while you help point the client in the right direction. Likewise, phone consults give clients time to ask you about some specifics they have in their mind (e.g., Did you think it was funny when . . . ? Does the twist work for you? What if I took out this character?). The drawback is that these clients don't get that written report; they have to take notes from your conversation, but then again, they're only picking and choosing those comments that work best for them. You might also consider offering a combination of notes and phone consultation. Establish beforehand how many hours you plan to offer for your fee and a plan for if you go over that time. Again, phone consults are more in depth than coverage and you should make sure you are compensated accordingly.

Your experience with story analysis may also help you branch away from the freelance sector into full-time employment with a production company, studio, agency, or management company as an industry assistant, story editor, creative executive, or director of development. It is not so easy or common to jump into one of the latter three without first paying one's dues in an administrative capacity, but your work portfolio and story sense should help you to at least break in and will probably benefit your climb through the ranks of a company.

I have also seen many readers go on to become working writers. Michael Gilvary, for instance, used to read scripts for me (and various others) and went on to become a professional screenwriter for companies such as Paramount and Intermedia. He says, "There is no better crash course in screenwriting than working as a reader for a studio or production company. When you're wading through hundreds of script submissions and distilling them into snack-size chunks, you learn very quickly what makes a story take flight, and what makes one crash and burn."

The bold risk-taker might attempt to bypass the midlevel and head straight for the top as a producer or manager. Seeing how yours could become the first set of professional eyes to read through a property, you might be granted a slight competitive edge over the rest of the industry. If the project is not already owned by another entity and there's something you like about it, you could be the first to approach a writer or director client about securing the rights and coming onboard as a producer. For better or worse, the meaning of "Producer" has been diluted in the past number of years. In the traditional sense, a producer will help to secure financing for a project and see it through from development all the way to theatrical release and beyond. Certainly, if you have enough of a background to serve a property in this capacity, there's no reason why you shouldn't aim for a Producer role. But nowadays, many producers (including executive, coproducers, and associate producers) are credited for a lesser contribution to the realization of a film or TV project. One may have just been responsible for a portion of the financing, another may have at one point owned the rights to the story idea, and another may have simply called up an A-List actor friend to ask him to read the material, resulting in that talent's attachment to the project. In any event, as a story analyst on the front lines, you will have developed the skill with which to identify strong material and, if you have the time, energy, resources, finances, luck, and patience, you might be able to take such experience with you on your producing endeavors.

Some readers might tap into so many fresh, unrepresented writers that they consider hanging up a shingle as a literary manager. Literary managers are similar to agents in that they seek out raw talent whose scripts possess great commercial potential, sign them to a contract, and then try to interest buyers or attachments in their clients' scripts. By law, managers cannot structure the formal deal for a script purchase the way an agent does, but increasingly, managers are also serving as producers on projects. Hence, not only do they take a percentage for their client's sale, but they also garner a producer's fee for however small or large a role they assume in the production.

The descriptions for producers and managers are relatively simple and might make it seem as if anyone can just jump in as one or the other. But there are various legal intricacies involved in both professions, and if you truly aspire to either, it is recommended that you consult with an accountant, a lawyer, and others in the field. Furthermore, surviving as a successful manager or producer requires an enormous amount of networking. You may have a hot client with a hot property, but it's a useless situation if you don't have anyone to sell to. Such networking, in turn, requires a great amount of time and expense.

Staying Current and Looking to the Future

As the work pours in, it will behoove you to stay on top of what's hip, what's hot, and what's not. Remember, clients usually appreciate it if you compare/contrast their submission with a produced film or two in your commercial potential and comments sections. Doing so will require that you possess as many films in your "memory banks" as possible. Part of the advice, then, is obvious: see as many films as you can. Get out there to the theaters to see current releases; head to the video store or subscribe to Netflix for stacks of DVDs. Not too difficult, seeing how you wouldn't be reading scripts if you didn't love to watch movies, right?

But here is where it might take a little more effort on your part: make sure not to limit yourself to those types of movies that you prefer, because you won't always be reading scripts in those genres that attract you. Don't care for loud, violent action flicks? Can't bear to sit and read subtitles for a small, indie art house film? Suck it up! You must be up on what works, what doesn't work, and why for those projects as much as for any other genre. Furthermore, see older films—not just those from the past five years. Inevitably, you will come across a script that pays homage to (or borrows a little too much from) a movie of yesteryear. Occasionally, impress your client by conjuring up a classic.

(Check out the American Film Institute's top 100 list for many of them.) Some examples of language you might use: "Whereas in *Citizen Kane*, Charles Kane is a decent man at his core, this character has no sympathetic qualities"; "Structurally, this script takes a *Rashomon* approach to storytelling"; "The author seems to take the basics behind *The Good, the Bad and the Ugly* and set it in fourteenth-century England." To be able to make such helpful statements, you will have to know classic films.

Another important component to staying on top of tastes and trends is to monitor regularly the trade magazines *Variety, The Hollywood Reporter*, and *Screen International*, which will often tell you who's buying what and what's in development and production where. Film magazines such as *Premiere* and *Entertainment Weekly* and some major newspapers will give you "sneak peeks," gossip, and buzz regarding upcoming releases. For a hipper alternative, *Ain't It Cool News* (*www.aintitcoolnews.com*) promises to give you the skinny. The site *scriptsales.com* lists just that on a daily basis and includes a logline, genre, and the buyer.

Stay current with the methodology of story analysis itself. Be sure to track the continued growth of technology, as it will inevitably affect how you pursue and expedite your workload in the near future. PDAs and cell phones have entered the mainstream and dictate how we conduct our business and lives. Perhaps it will become the norm for us to read scripts off of our Blackberries, iPods, or with the help of Verizon Wireless. If possible, keep in touch with other story analysts to hear in what ways they are using technology to make things easier for their clients, and vice versa. Certainly, there is nothing wrong with becoming a pioneer yourself and adding your own innovation to the process.

In addition to tracking *how* material is being analyzed, it will benefit you to track *what* is being analyzed. The utilization of story analysis is currently extending from its traditional base of feature film and television into more technology-inspired content. Short film showcases on the Internet such as Triggerstreet.com and Atom Films and cable stations such as the Independent Film Channel have spawned wide interest and a strong outlet for aspiring filmmakers. With the exponential rise in demand for DVD and other forms of home entertainment such as Video on Demand, Internet streaming/downloading, iPods and cell phones, we are seeing additional programming and new forms of filmed entertainment created for these media, such as one- to ten-minute narrative "featurettes," "Webisodes," or "mobisodes." With the call for short films and these new forms of storytelling also comes the need for the scripts on which to base these projects and, thus, the need for feedback on those scripts.

The video game is a media form that is also taking the entertainment market by storm. Successful games are grossing as much as, if not more than, successful feature films. With the explosion of interest in this technology by both investors and consumers comes the mandate for more intricate story lines. Therefore, more involved game scripts are being written—many with the same regard for basic storytelling elements as features and television. In fact, some screenwriters are beginning to cross over into the game world, while those universities that teach game technologies, such as Carnegie Mellon University, are adding a creative writing facet to their programs. As is the case with film and television, a good game starts with a good script. And if there are scripts, there is the need for someone to read them, meaning that games could very well represent a lucrative new playing field for the expert in story analysis.

Appendix A: Coverage Examples

The following three samples are real coverage by real working readers. Note that the third sample (*Dear Zoe,*) is coverage for a novel, thus has a longer synopsis.

FLAG FILMS COVERAGE

TITLE:	GENERATION WRECKS	DATE:	11/20/05
AUTHOR:	Xxxxx Xxxxx	SUBMITTED TO:	Xxxx Xxxxxx
GENRE:	Drama	SUB BY:	Xxxxxx Xxx
CIRCA:	Present	FORM:	Screenplay
LOCALE:	San Francisco, Northern CA coast	PAGES:	122
ANALYST:	AZ		

PREMISE: During a business retreat, a young, straightlaced insurance salesman gives refuge to a couple of drifters in his motel room.

BUDGET: Low

CHARACTERIZATIONS:	C
DIALOGUE:	C
STRUCTURE:	D
STORY UNIQUENESS:	D
SETTING UNIQUENESS:	C

(Letter Grade: A through F)

PROJECT RECOMMEND:	PASS
WRITER RECOMMEND:	PASS

SYNOPSIS

ZACH (26) works in San Francisco as a low-level insurance sales-man within a large corporation. Due in part to his workaholic nature, he has found himself in an unfulfilling relationship with girlfriend SUSAN (20s). Zach and his obnoxious friend, PETE (20s), head out of town to the coastal village of Seal Point, California, for a company staff retreat. Unfortunately, there was a mix-up and there aren't any rooms left, leaving Zach and Pete to check into separate rooms in a dingy, roadside motel.

On the night before their retreat begins, Zach ditches Pete to go for a stroll alone on the wharf. There, he runs into an earthy, hemp-garbed free spirit, LUCKY (23), who is photographing some seals that rest on the docks. They engage in some conversation, and Lucky reveals that she's traveling cross-country with a friend named STACEY. Zach, intrigued by this nomadic soul, invites Lucky to dinner at the nearby diner where Lucky shares that she and Stacey were both arrested for shoplifting a small amount of produce from a local market; they're stuck in town until their hear-ing on Monday. Stacey, it turns out, is a guy and he's in a jail cell (there's only room for men at the jail right now). Lucky plans on sleeping in her Jeep. When a storm hits, however, Zach offers her a roof over her head at his motel room.

At Zach's room, as they settle in, Pete knocks on the door, wasted, and sees Lucky. After Zach gets rid of him, Zach drinks scotch and extols its virtues. Lucky makes a pass at him, but they can't quite find the connection.

The next day, Pete doesn't remember a thing about any girl, so there's no risk there with Susan. Zach introduces himself in a work-shop group only to find Lucky waving for him. In the hallway, she tells him she needs some bail money. She would use the emer-gency credit card given to her by her dad, but she'd rather not. Begrudged, Zach shells out everything he has and makes her promise to vacate the room. At the conclusion of the day, however, Zach arrives back at his room to find scrawny, peevish STACEY (23) getting stoned on his bed with Lucky. Zach resists at first and asks them to leave, but the secondhand smoke overcomes him and he climbs on board for their night of fun. Zach does manage to sneak away to speak with Susan, who appears to be a manic stress-ball. She refuses Zach's invitation to come stay with him for the rest of the week.

The following morning, Lucky and Stacey announce that they're stuck in town for at least one more day—their Jeep is shot (or is it, Zach wonders). Zach permits them to stay one more night, but he decides to kick them out when Pete bumps into the three of them and Stacey roughs him up. Later, Lucky apologizes to Zach and convinces him to join them in a get-together on the beach with some fellow "travelers." Lucky admits to Zach that she stole some money from her father before leaving her hometown of Rochester. Zach tries to convince her to call her dad before it's too late. By dawn, Zach is completely obliterated and, in his haze, begs Lucky and Stacey to take him with them on the road.

Back at the hotel, Zach again invites them in, but only if Stacey apologizes to Pete. Stacey does. But it's too late—Pete has been talking to Susan about Zach's odd behavior and his two freeload-ers. When Zach is out of the room (getting ice for more scotch), Susan calls; Lucky picks up the phone.

Toward the conclusion of the company retreat, Lucky and Stacey are finally ready to hit the open road. Their vehicle is back in action, and the fond farewell begins. Lucky admits to Zach that she might ditch Stacey soon and head home to her father to make things right. After the duo depart, Susan finds Zach on the wharf, right where he met Lucky. She's far from the shrew that we had imagined (in various cutaways). Rather, she's quite rational and together. Still, she is suspicious and angry enough to ask about the woman who answered Zach's phone. Pete suddenly pops in on them to report that he just saw Lucky and Stacey breaking into Zach's room.

Zach, Susan, and Pete rush to the room, convinced that Zach has been wiped clean. What they find, however, is a bottle of scotch and a thank-you note for Zach's hospitality. Zach tells Susan the truth about everything, and Susan is actually touched by it all. They realize how off-track they have gotten and agree to work harder on their relationship.

BRIEF

This well-intentioned drama makes a grab for the hearts of twenty-something audiences who are on the verge of choosing their own life paths, but its lack of conflict and talky characters make for a generally ineffective narrative.

COMMENTS

As this story begins, we latch on to Zach, who is a likable enough main character—a yuppie on the corporate fast-track who yearns for more (more meaning, more youth, more time, perhaps). And once Zach latches on to free-spirited Lucky, the true potential of the script becomes apparent. Unfortunately, the author never fully achieves that potential. This small story goes wrong due to its ultimately loose structure, verbose scene work, and soft tension.

In terms of structure and plot, one wonders what the central thread is. Sure, Zach's character arc is visible. From the moment we see this overworked, anal-retentive guy in an unhappy relationship with his girlfriend, we know where he is and where he's going, especially when Lucky shows up. And yes, this is a character-driven piece, but it would greatly help pacing if the narrative were shaped by some other superficial motor outside of the Zach/Lucky relationship. As written, the script suffers from a profound lack of conflict and stakes. Zach's schedule from meeting to meeting meanders along about as lazily as Lucky and Stacey do through their daily life. Perhaps things would be ratcheted up if it were Zach's big week in which to prove himself to his superiors in the hopes of a major promotion. But every time Zach tries to make a move in the career direction, there are Lucky and Stacey to pull him the opposite way.

It would also be nice to see Zach do more with Lucky and Stacey from scene to scene. Currently, these characters spend far too much time sitting in the motel room, sitting on the beach, sitting in a diner—simply talking. Zach talks about his frustrations, but never truly exhibits them in his actions. Likewise, we learn about Lucky's regrets with her parents, but most of her dialogue amounts to a laundry list of verbal quirks and by-the-numbers hippy-girl chat. The story is set up for some great situational conflict (and humor) that the writer never cashes in on. What if Lucky were to end up at a formal function by Zach's side? What if Zach were actually swooped away by some of Lucky's fellow tribe-sters for a spell? What if Susan showed up in Seal Point earlier?

Speaking of Susan, the author's use of her character is nearly inde-cipherable. One moment we see her on the phone with Zach, under a table, having a meltdown. The next moment, she's an ele-gant princess. At one point she's Zach's capable therapist, then she's about to slit her wrists. The aim here is most likely to coax us into one impression of Susan, only to present a twist at the end as she emerges as something utterly different. In more capable hands, there could be some humor in all the inconsistency, but in this draft, Susan simply appears to be all over the map without rhyme or reason.

While it is somewhat refreshing that Zach and Lucky stop just short of any real romance (thus rendering some bittersweet overtones), the story also stops short in some unfortunate ways. Essentially, the writer appears hesitant to commit to anything. Lucky is sort of a hippy . . . but she's also a suburban daddy's girl at heart. Zach sort of enjoys his yuppie existence . . . but then again, he wants something else. Zach is on his company retreat to work hard . . . but we never see him doing so. Susan, as mentioned, is psychotic and dragging Zach down . . . but she's also understanding and supportive. Whereas all of these characters and their situations begin at a sort of middle ground, this story might benefit if the author employed some extremes and then eased the characters into these moderate areas by the story's end.

At the end of the day, GENERATION WRECKS appears to be a story about trust and the pursuit of one's bliss. It's a nice notion, but the insides of this particular script emerge as too scattered for lack of a tighter, more streamlined skeleton.

PASS.

STORY DEPARTMENT COVERAGE

TITLE:	HIGHER GROUND	ANALYST:	Xxxxxxx
AUTHOR:	Xxxxxxx	DATE COVERED:	6/6/03
FORM:	Screenplay	# PAGES:	113
DRAFT:	First	PERIOD:	The future
GENRE:	Sci-Fi/Action	SETTING:	Far-off planets/space

ELEMENTS: Xxxxxxx to star; Xxxxxxx to direct

LOGLINE: A human, interplanetary miner headed back to earth after years of service is accidentally stranded en route. He must simultaneously battle and trust members of two races of aliens to survive.

COMMERCIAL POTENTIAL: Packed with action, gunfights, and one man's struggle to overcome the mistakes his race has created, this piece might locate some appeal in the youth market. However, lacking a novel twist or strong visual interpretation, it could just as easily fail to rise above the genre to stake its own claim. Potential large budget is a factor.

PREMISE:	Fair
PLOT:	Fair-Good
STRUCTURE:	Fair-Good
CHARACTERS:	Good
DIALOGUE:	Good
BUDGET:	HIGH

SYNOPSIS

In another solar system, JOHN CARRICK, 26, works in the water mines of a desolate planet alongside a humanoid and human-raised species/race called the Truxuns, who are the descendents of life of Mars. Despite the fact that they're both working in the same mine, the two races are segregated because of deep-seated animosity mirroring interracial tension. On his last day of a three-year tour of duty in a grueling mine, John saves lives of both races as the mine suddenly floods. On an accelerated schedule to depart for Earth due to an incoming meteor shower, John hitches a ride with a PILOT in his Greyhound bus-like spaceship. A mass of Truxuns forms outside the ship, wanting to join John to Earth, but due to overpopulation there, any further Truxun immigration has been declared illegal, even though humans created them.

After the pilot discovers a fault (and possible sabotage) with the ship, they're forced to land on planet Prikeston 9, which is full of Truxuns. Once colonized by humans, the planet and most of its resources have since been controlled by Truxuns. Meanwhile, in a nearby settlement, a Truxun named MASTIG is making a romantic move on his wife, NISHTA, until they're interrupted by the unwelcome humans. Mastig appears, and the pilot offers Mastig a form of pay for fuel barrels. Meanwhile, John notices the attractive Nishta. After Mastig turns the pilot down, the latter begins to antagonize Mastig and finally draws on him. A shoot-out ensues, and the pilot shoots Mastig dead. In the battle, the pilot is also shot to death, while John barely escapes.

John tries to make it out of the settlement, but runs into Nishta. She takes pity on him and lets him go free. At the same time, two Truxuns named KROM and VEE rally other male Truxuns to hunt the human. John tries to escape the settlement, but lands in the middle of the Truxun hunters. Just as they're about to execute John, a small army of human resistance FIGHTERS surprises the Truxuns.

A melee begins, which allows John to escape. He makes it to a nearby stone observatory, where he runs into Nishta again. John ties her up, not feeling he can trust her. Nishta explains how Mastig was her husband and "Goac," or community leader, and that Vee is his brother. Now that Mastig is dead, she legally belongs to Vee.

Meanwhile in a basement, Vee talks to a huge beast called a LOK'PHONT, who is being held prisoner. The beast has overheard the commotion above ground, and Vee explains what has transpired. The beast, jailed for an attempt to heist Truxun supplies, claims he can catch the human for him. He gives Vee his sacred pendant as collateral to ensure his return after he kills the human. Vee and the other Truxuns release the beast, who goes bounding after the runaway human. The Lok'phont soon begins firing at the observatory door and creeps up on an opening, but John tricks him and shoots him dead.

Back down in the settlement, the Truxuns can't believe the human has killed the deadly beast. Suddenly, Nishta appears to them and screams out that she's being held hostage. Vee gets riled up, arms himself, and prepares to scale the hill to confront the human by himself. Unbeknownst to the Truxuns, the dead beast's pendant has emitted a distress signal, which alerts three Lok'phont spaceships in the area. The LOK'PHONT PILOT leads the ships toward Prikeston 9. Back on the planet, Vee creeps toward the observatory, not aware that sidekick Krom is leading about fifteen Truxuns toward the target from the opposite side. One of the Truxun snipers jumps the gun and begins shooting at John. He misses, but the other Truxuns begin storming the observatory. John dispatches most of them, but his leg is injured in the process. Vee and Krom both retreat back to the settlement but have surrounded the place.

John decides to use his mining skills and a laser tool to dig himself and Nishta a back way out of there. Two subterranean dragons spring from their newly formed opening, forcing John and Nishta to battle and slay both. After the dust settles, John and Nistha make love. Later, the Lok'phont ships land, but one of them is destroyed by the storm. The Lok'phont pilot and his crew decide to wait out the storm inside their ship. Meanwhile, Vee and Krom send robot carrier birds with explosives to destroy the observatory dome. After several charges explode, Vee and Krom believe they've killed John and Nishta. However, they spot John in an opening. They send up more robotic birds, but this time John defends the structure with a homemade weapon. John is proud of himself and yells defiant and derogatory remarks down at the Truxuns. Nishta finally realizes she doesn't want to die in the observatory with a human and returns to the settlement. John later finds a holographic picture of Nishta's father, the observatory's human creator, which Nishta left behind. After rejoining the settlement, Vee senses Nishta's infidelity with the human and spits on her. She is banished from the settlement only to be taken prisoner by the Lok'phonts.

Meanwhile, the Truxuns have rebuilt the transport as a warship with plans to use it on John and then, perhaps, to overtake the resources of weaker settlements. Later, the Lok'phonts torture Nishta with a tarantula-like creature. Before it bites, she finally reveals that their beast-brother was murdered by a human, John. The Lok'phonts want revenge. Vee pilots the warship up to the observatory and begins to raze it. John takes refuge in the tunnel. Suddenly, a reconnaissance Lok'phont ship appears and signals Vee's ship. They want to know what happened to their brother, revealing that they have Nishta in their possession. Vee tries to explain what happened and that the human killed their brother. However, the Lok'phont pilot claims they're still getting their brother's distress signal—and the source is the warship. Vee suddenly understands as he pulls out the beast's pendant—which is blinking. The two ships entangle. Meanwhile, Krom is on foot and finds John in the observatory. The two grapple outside, and finally John is able to pitch the Truxun over the cliff side to his death.

While the ships duke it out, Nishta struggles to wrench free of her bonds. John manages to rappel onto the Lok'phont ship and rescue Nishta. They defeat the Lok'phont pilot, but Vee comes at them in the warship. As the two ships tangle, Vee jumps aboard the Lok'phont ship just before his warship crashes to the ground among the settlement. As John battles Vee, Nishta sets the tarantula animal loose on Vee—and it mortally bites him in the neck. Not knowing how to pilot the Lok'phont ship, they crash-land outside the settlement. John returns her father's picture to her. They find the Lok'phont mother ship, which is John's ticket back to earth, but Nishta won't be able to join him. Before John leaves, Nishta views a message from her dead father, which was hidden in back of the picture. He reveals that he hid supplies in the hills for her in the event of an emergency. Nishta rides into the hills to find the supplies; John decides to join her for the time being.

COMMENTS

An adventurous, romantic, and suspenseful actioner about a human miner who's trying to get home to earth but ends up battling spiteful and vindictive aliens. This story recalls such films as *Enemy Mine* and others that deal with aliens on a deeper, more dramatic level. The story is somewhat entertaining and has some suspenseful elements.

John Carrick is the everyman underling who takes on heroic stature in his battle against the vindictive Truxuns. Stranded on Prikeston 9, he winds up under siege with a beautiful alien, Nishta. Recalling *Romeo and Juliet*, John and Nishta are the two unlikely lovers who find themselves trapped in the observatory. Throughout most of the second act, they are under siege in this building, and their romance provides the personal drama meant to compensate for the violence and bloodshed in the interim. John provides a fairly good heroic character, and we can easily relate to his apolitical stand on the conflict between the two races.

Nishta is a sympathetic female lead, and her character is also developed to a significant degree. Vee is an adequate "villain" and does provide some logical if somewhat melodramatic conflict for John. However, the relationship between Vee and Nishta could stand to be tighter: What if Vee were just as attractive to Nishta as John seems to be? This would make her decision-making process more difficult and thus heighten her inner conflict.

There are some story flaws that should be mentioned. For one thing, the whole backstory regarding the humans versus the Truxuns seems superfluous. The political conflict doesn't have that much bearing on the present story. The writer might think about just having John wander into this alien community and then suffer the consequences of his pilot's racism. Despite the liberal genre the writer has chosen, there are also a few credibility issues. The building of the warship is one of the more puzzling elements in the script. Why would the Truxuns bother building a ship when they could just bomb the heck out of the observatory? The only reason for building a ship (in Vee's mind) would be to rescue Nishta. However, this angle isn't logical anymore because he forsook her already. Also, one wonders why the Truxuns don't just starve John out. If they laid in wait around the perimeter, either John or Nishta would have to venture out for some kind of sustenance.

The Lok'phonts are certainly interesting creatures, but the story seems to keep them on the backburner after the initial beast dies. If this is a rescue mission, it doesn't seem feasible that a windstorm would keep them from looking for their comrade. This turn of events makes the showdown between the warship and the cruiser a bit forced and coincidental.

The action scenes are nicely detailed and eloquent. The writer has done a decent job of creating suspense through the characters' actions and also the battle sequences. The carrier robots are a nice touch in particular—and convert to an interesting weapon. The battles between John and the Truxuns are also handled nicely, with

John using the mining weapon as his trump card. The dialogue is concise and meaningful in the context of its drama but could use a little more depth in terms of its emotional range.

This interesting and somewhat promising science-fiction story has some workable elements but needs more tweaking, especially with regard to the story structure and certain developments in the plot. The characters, dialogue, and action are substantial and competent enough to warrant consideration and pursuit of another solid draft attempt.

PROJECT: Consider

WRITER: Consider

TITLE:	DEAR ZOE,	ACCOUNT #:	N/A
AUTHOR:	Philip Beard	ANALYST #:	21
FORM:	Novel	DATE COVERED:	March 20, 2005
# PAGES:	196	DRAFT:	© 2005 Viking
GENRE:	Drama	PERIOD:	Present
SETTING:	Pittsburgh		

LOGLINE: A fifteen-year-old Pittsburgh girl comes to terms with the accidental death of her younger sister—a death for which she holds herself responsible and that occurred by coincidence on 9/11/01.

PROJECT: Recommend
WRITER: Recommend

COMMENT SUMMARY: Not since Chappie (a.k.a. Bone) in Russell Banks' RULE OF THE BONE has there been a teenage narrator as powerful, raw, brutally honest, and real as Tess DeNuzio in DEAR ZOE,. Tess's fight to come to terms with the death of her younger sister, her struggle through adolescence and into womanhood carrying the weight of such tragedy, becomes a breathtaking insight into grief and healing—and the strength it takes to carry on.

COMMERCIAL POTENTIAL: DEAR ZOE, brings to mind such films as IN AMERICA and THE SWEET HEREAFTER. A powerful study of grief and loss told from the point of view of a fifteen-year-old girl, this film will have a major impact with the intelligent film-going audience in the art house arena. There is the potential to reach a wider adolescent audience as well.

(X)	EXCELLENT	GOOD	FAIR	POOR
CONCEPT	X			
STORYLINE	X			
CHARACTERS	X			
DIALOGUE	X			
BUDGET	HIGH __	MEDIUM __	LOW __X	

SYNOPSIS

From the novel's very first sentence, *I have memories of you before you were even born*, we understand that fifteen-year-old TESS DENUZIO is addressing her narrative to one very specific person. We soon learn that what is about to unravel is a letter written by Tess to her little sister, ZOE, after Zoe's sudden and accidental death on September 11, 2001—far from the wreckage in New York and Washington.

Tess lives with her mother, ELLY, her stepfather, DAVID, and her other younger sister EMILY. Zoe and Emily are Tess's half-sisters. Tess's real father and Elly had separated long ago. Tess remembers sitting around the kitchen table with her mother and David, tossing out different names to committee for their approval. The family decides on the name Zoe because they don't know anyone else who has it. Tess's mom feels that this will lead her to be unique and independent. We learn a bit about David, who is the responsible suit-and-tie type of dad, and about Tess's real father, NICK, who is sort of a well-intentioned deadbeat, a lovable loser.

While it appears that life has moved on after Zoe's death, the family is actually falling apart. It's been less than a year since the incident, and Tess anticipates the first anniversary of their tragedy and how hard it will be. Tess explains how the family has seen a therapist—how the doctor had told her that her mom and David had excluded her from their grief. Tess reveals that what she really wanted to ask the doctor was, "Why shouldn't the loss of someone you love ruin you?"

Tess's mother is particularly affected, as she spirals into deep depression. She can barely get herself up off the couch to do anything anymore. Tess and David now share responsibility for the care of Emily, who is six years old and in first grade. It doesn't help that Tess takes two and a half hours to get ready in the morning. Tess explains how she thought about taking her own life once, after Zoe died, and how Emily caught her in the bathroom with her mom's pills and seemed to know. Emily has always been so grown up for such a young girl. She seems to be the strongest of them all.

Tess's mom paints over the walls in Zoe's bedroom one day. There had been Peter Rabbit characters stenciled and painted on those walls. Tess and her mom had spent a whole day painting the characters there for Zoe. Now, without asking, she has decided to paint over them in a dull beige color. Tess comes home to the smell of paint and is shocked. She rushes up to Zoe's room and sees her mom crying and shaking, paint roller in her hand. Tess stands outside the door and weeps. David comes home and is furious.

Tess discovers that her mom has sought comfort in JUSTIN, their local grocery clerk. In a moment of sheer vulnerability and honesty, Elly says to her, "Tess, you can't always get comfort from people who have the same pain as you have." Tess can't bear to live in her own house and decides to move in with Nick, her real dad. He lives in a shady part of town, hardly works, and drives a beat-up old mail truck (the UPS kind). He is a well-intentioned and likable guy, though. Tess loves him unconditionally.

Tess's dad has never been able to get himself together since he and Elly split. He goes from job to job, but always manages to find an excuse to quit. He has a couple of German Shepherds around the house, and the biggest one, KEISHA, has just given birth to a litter of puppies. He'll sell them for extra cash. The runt of the litter, though, a little guy with a white stripe over one of his eyes, takes a liking to Tess. Tess names him FRANK.

Tess and her father fall into a routine. He drives her to school and picks her up. He works out at the gym most of the day and makes a few deliveries with the truck now and then. Just when things get comfortable, Tess realizes that she's left Emily at home all alone. She hasn't even thought about Emily in a while. She decides to see Emily for the first time since she left and waits for her outside her school. Emily asks if she's coming home, and Tess says no. Tess tells Emily that her leaving had nothing to do with her. Emily knows. Tess and her dad drive Emily home for the first time. Tess promises her that they will see each other every day after school and that she and her dad will drive her home.

Tess soon begins to notice Nick's cute eighteen-year-old next-door neighbor, JIMMY FREEZE. She sees him coming in and out of his house all the time and tries to get him to notice her. He doesn't, or so she thinks. One day Tess baits him over to her porch and they exchange words for the first time. The feeling is electric, on both sides. Tess tries to get him a beer but Nick chases him away.

A shady guy named TRAVIS stops by the house one day while Tess sits on the porch. He drops a wad of cash for Tess's dad. At this point Tess becomes aware that her dad is dealing drugs. Her dad arrives and tries to explain himself. He explains that he only sells weed to adults, nothing stronger. If someone's going to do it, it might as well be him. Tess acts more like the parent here, scolding him but ultimately giving in. Later, Jimmy climbs through Tess's window, and they share a joint. Her first. Since her dad's dealing it she might as well try it, right? Jimmy and Tess kiss for the first time. Getting high with Jimmy and kissing him for hours will also become a part of Tess's routine.

Tess and her dad pick up Emily on the last day of school and Emily is upset. It's not fair that she has to miss both Zoe and Tess at the same time. No one thinks of Emily. No one thinks she misses Zoe. Now that school's over, when will she see Tess? Tess holds her in her lap and hugs her tight. When Tess and her father drop Emily off at home, Tess can't so much as even look at the house let alone her stepfather David. David makes small talk and asks how she's doing. Avoiding a response, she digs her foot at a hole in the floor of the rusted-out old mail truck and actually puts her foot right through it. Her dad has to help her pull it out.

Jimmy opens up to Tess and tells her about his mother dying of cancer. Tess still can't tell him about Zoe. She doesn't feel right that she hasn't told him, but she simply can't. Jimmy gets Tess a summer job at Kennywood, the local amusement park. Jimmy works the Skycoaster and Tess works at Thelma's Frozen Lemonade stand. Although she's desperately afraid of it, Jimmy and Tess finally ride the Skycoaster together, and *right there, suspended in mid air, hundreds of feet above the Earth*, Jimmy tells her he loves her. She loves him, too.

Tess and her mom talk occasionally, but it's difficult. Her mother slowly seems to be getting better. They talk about how it used to be just the two of them, before David and Emily, and how close they were. At one point, her mom tries to justify her time with Justin. Tess now understands how she could have sought comfort outside of their circle of grief, what with her newfound relationship with Jimmy. Tess's mom tells her that she feels she is losing her and that she just can't bear to lose both of them, both Zoe and Tess. Tess tries to tell her mom that she's not losing her, but her mom is not so sure. Elly asks her to come home for her sixteenth birthday. Tess is uncertain about it.

Tess runs into Emily and David at Kennywood. It's awkward. Emily gives her the silent treatment. David invites Tess to dinner with him and Emily and her mom. She says that she already has plans.

Nick gets busted for dealing drugs the day before Tess's sixteenth birthday. Jimmy is with him, too. That's how Jimmy knew her dad! Tess spends the night alone at her dad's and has a terrible nightmare about Zoe's death. She wakes up alone the next day and she's sixteen. Nick calls from jail and says that she and Jimmy have to get the truck out of hock and will be home shortly. Jimmy whispers something to him; Nick says happy birthday.

Elly shows up unannounced to see Tess and wish her happy birthday. She gives Tess a few gifts. It's a moment of reconciliation.

For the first time in a long time Tess is really happy to see her. Eventually, Tess convinces her mom to leave, however, because her dad and Jimmy are on the way home and she doesn't want her mom to find out that her dad was busted. At the same time, she really doesn't want her to go.

Tess's dad and Jimmy arrive. Frank (the German Shepherd pup) runs out after the truck. Nick hits Frank with the mail truck. This time it's different though; there is sound. When Zoe was killed by an oncoming car, Tess didn't hear a thing. Everything went completely silent. Tess's dad rushes Frank off to the vet.

Tess and Jimmy go upstairs to her room. She lies in his arms awhile and cries as he comforts her. Suddenly they find themselves kissing and, for the first time, doing more. Jimmy certainly knows what he's doing and Tess loves it at first. As soon as he enters her, though, Tess begins to weep. She has an overwhelming feeling of guilt—guilt for allowing herself to feel such pleasure. She cries harder and begins to shake. She begins to really freak and it freaks Jimmy too. He rolls off of her and she screams at him to get out. She buries herself under the covers and folds herself up into the fetal position. After some time, Tess suddenly feels a hand on her shoulder from under the covers and realizes that Jimmy is still there. He hasn't left her. He stayed to comfort her.

Tess decides to tell him everything about Zoe. Tess recounts the story of exactly what happened the day Zoe died, in precise detail. From this sight of Zoe flying in the air and landing in the soft grass to the thump-thump-thump sound of the gurney as it rolled her into the hospital, she tells it all exactly as she experienced it. And how she was supposed to be watching her little sister when it happened.

Tess then says how she thinks of all the people who died that day, September 11, but not because of that day. How their pain and grief have somehow been minimized and overshadowed by that tragic event. She thinks about the people who have had the misfortune of being born on that day too—how awkward it is for them when they have to tell people their birth date.

Nick calls and Frank is OK. He's lucky. He's got a bump on the head and a broken leg, that's it. Tess and Jimmy discuss what just happened. Tess explains that nothing happened that she didn't want to happen. They are both OK with it.

Nick comes home exhausted and goes straight to bed. Tess can't sleep. She decides in the middle of the night that she absolutely must see a picture of Zoe right now. Her dad drives her to her house. She goes inside and looks for her favorite photo. It's not there, Emily must have it. It is at this exact moment that Tess realizes she's not going back with her dad. She's home. She slips into Emily's room. Emily asks her if she's going to stay, and she says yes. Tess goes to her dad in the truck and tells him that she's staying. Her dad tells her that she can keep Frank. Elly sobs the next morning when she walks into Emily's room and sees Tess sleeping in bed with her. Tess is home.

COMMENTS

There hasn't been a voice this real, this emotive, and this honest in contemporary literature in quite some time. It is without doubt a remarkable feat by the writer to achieve such a transcendent insight into suffering from a fifteen-year-old girl. Mr. Beard has given us a coming-of-age novel that will leave its mark indelibly on the conscious of its readers, both young and old. In Tess, Mr. Beard has defined the young antihero of a generation; she is truly a female Holden Caulfield.

Perhaps what makes Tess so unique and compelling is the honesty with which she shares her grief and her confusion. When she poses the question, "Why shouldn't the loss of someone you love ruin you?" we are floored. Haven't we all dealt with this question on some level but have been afraid to ask? And how can a fifteen-year-old girl so perfectly and succinctly summarize thoughts that have been spinning in the heads of wiser men for generations? Considering the amount of thought it provokes, the economy of words in this question is sublime. We spend our entire time with Tess trying to find the answer. We are immediately drawn to Tess through this one simple question. Such intimacy has been created with such few words. And those words aren't even supposed to be for us; they are supposed to be for Tess and for Zoe alone. Tess including us in this letter to her sister somehow makes us feel a part of her. It is a powerful choice by the writer. Unlike so many other astute characters in literature and film that seem to go for a witty and sarcastic flamboyance (Ignatius J. Reilly in A CONFED-ERACY OF DUNCES comes to mind), Tess doesn't pretend to know anything. She does know loss, though, and she's taking us along with her on her journey of acceptance and understanding.

That said, how will this intimacy translate on screen? There are so many thoughts and feelings that Tess shares with Zoe (and us) through words that she doesn't share with the outside world. This will be the primary hurdle in adapting the novel for film. How can these heartfelt perceptions be translated without blatant exposition and voice-over narrative? The answer is that this novel is ripe and fertile with cinematic moments, and the novel is structured in a way that gives these moments maximum impact. For example, we only get glimpses of the day that Zoe was killed at the very end, when Tess is compelled to recount that day for Jimmy. At this point the tension is enormous; we are riveted. Tess doesn't just want to relive that day—she *needs* to relive that day. As an audience, we don't just want to see that day—we *need* to see that day. The writer has ever so carefully built up our compassion and love for Tess, and we need to travel to that painful past with her. This will work well on film.

Another reason that this novel will work well on film is that the conflict is both internal and external and is ever present. There are scenes when the characters collide like atoms. Each encounter between Tess and her mother, father, stepfather, and sister carries such enormous tension. Each encounter between Tess and Jimmy carries such weight too. In short, the interactions between Tess and those around her are heartbreaking and real. The dialogue itself cuts to your soul. Scenes such as Tess's mother painting over the walls in Zoe's room, Tess and Emily's conversation outside Emily's school when Tess first sees her after leaving home, Tess's mother arriving for her sixteenth birthday, Tess losing her virginity to Jimmy and not feeling like she deserves it—these are just a few of the scenes that are overwhelming and unforgettable.

This is a meaningful and important story, one that should be told. Tess's fight to come to terms with the death of her younger sister, her struggle through adolescence and into womanhood carrying the weight of such tragedy, becomes a breathtaking insight into grief and healing—and the strength it takes to carry on. The integrity with which Tess tells her story, the grace with which she pens her words, draws us into her immediately. We root for her to rescue herself, but somehow she seems to rescue us instead.

In short, there is the potential for this film to be unforgettable—to be as potent and devastating as the novel on which it is based.

Appendix B: Bibliography and Recommended Reading

Ackerman, Hal. *Write Screenplays That Sell: The Ackerman Way*. Los Angeles: Tallfellow Press, Inc., 2003.

Mason, Paul and Don Gold. *Producing for Hollywood*, 2nd Ed. New York: Allworth Press, 2004.

Campbell, Joseph. *The Hero with a Thousand Faces*. Princeton: Bollingen Series/Princeton University Press, 1973.

Field, Syd. *Screenplay: The Foundations of Screenwriting*. 3d ed. New York: Dell Publishing, 1979, 1982, 1994.

Goldman, William. *Adventures in the Screen Trade: A personal view of Hollywood and Screenwriting*. New York: Warner Books, 1983.

Herbert, Katherine Atwell. *The Perfect Screenplay: Writing It and Selling It*. New York: Allworth Press, 2006.

McKee, Robert. *Story*. New York: Regan Books, 1997.

Seger, Linda. *Making a Good Script Great*. 2d ed. Hollywood, California: Samuel French Trade, 1987, 1994.

Vogler, Christopher. *The Writer's Journey: Mythic Structure for Writers*. 2d ed. Studio City, California: Michael Wiese Productions, 1998.

Walter, Richard. *Screenwriting: The Art, Craft and Business of Film and Television Writing*. New York: Plume, 1988.

Wright, Kate. *Screenwriting Is Storytelling: Creating an A-List Screenplay That Sells*. New York: The Berkeley Publishing Group, 2004.

Appendix C: Where to Find Completed Screenplays for Practice

Not Produced

Triggerstreet, www.triggerstreet.com: Created by Kevin Spacey, this online hub for writers, readers, producers, and others gives you the opportunity to review new screenplays and offer much appreciated feedback to participants. If you're a writer, for every two scripts you review, you receive one review for your own material. Their tagline: "Help others, help yourself."

Simply Scripts, www.simplyscripts.com/unpro.html: This site provides access to several original, unproduced scripts.

Inktip, www.inktip.com: "Getting the right script into the right hands." This site is geared more toward screenwriters who wish to be read by producers. But if you qualify as a producer or company representative in the registration process and want to practice story analysis on unproduced material, this could be a good place to go for a wealth of new script listings.

Produced

Each of the sites below posts hundreds of produced scripts for anyone to look through and learn from.

Drew's Script-o-Rama, www.script-o-rama.com
Script Crawler, www.scriptcrawler.com
Script Secrets, www.scriptsecrets.net
Simply Scripts, www.simplyscripts.com

Appendix D: Other Resources for the Story Analyst

Research

American Film Institute, www.afi.com/tvevents/100years/ 100yearslist.htm: See "List of the 100 winning movies." Familiarize yourself with these classics!

BaselineFT, www.baseline.hollywood.com: This site offers a "Data-on-Demand information service" with deep archives on, among other things, cast and crew credits and box office history.

Box Office Mojo, www.boxofficemojo.com: The name speaks for itself.

Done Deal, www.scriptsales.com: This site offers current and archived script, treatment, pitch, and book sales.

HollywoodLitSales.com: This site offers archived spec script sales and more.

Internet Movie Database, www.imdb.com: Find news, reviews, credits, and box office information at this site. Premium subscriber service available (IMDb Pro).

Nielsen EDI, www.entdata.com: "The Worldwide Box Office Authority" offers analysis and other valuable data.

Show Biz Data, www.showbizdata.com: This site has development and production listings, industry news, box office grosses.

Thesaurus.com: Why look any further for that much-needed synonym?

VideoHound's Golden Movie Retriever (Farmington Hills, MI: Thomson Gale, 2007): This comprehensive, annual volume lists just about every film that has achieved any level of distribution. For a story analyst, the index by genre can also come in handy if you are having difficulty conjuring up a comparison for your client.

Consulting Advice

Getting Started in Consulting, by Alan Weiss, Ph.D. (New York: John Wiley & Sons, Inc., 2000), was shown to me by my sister-in-law, a Chicago economist, as I was beginning my company. I was surprised to find it quite relevant to the world of Hollywood story consulting.

Beverly Hills entertainment tax attorney Mitchell Miller can provide legal advice and support for independent contractors in the industry.

Mitchell R. Miller, Attorney at Law
315 South Beverly Drive, Suite 501
Beverly Hills, CA 90212
tel: 310-277-1848
fax: 310-551-1929
e-mail: mitchmiller@entertainmenttax.com

The Search for the Gig

Craigslist, www.craigslist.org: Los Angeles and New York are the best places to start. See "Film & TV Jobs," "Writing Jobs," and "Gigs" that fall under the "Creative" and "Writing" headings.

EntertainmentCareers.net: This site has job and internship listings.

Hollywood Creative Directory, www.hcdonline.com: This is the single best place to go for listings of producers, executives, agents, and managers—almost all of whom utilize script coverage.

Showbizjobs, www.showbizjobs.com: This site offers job and internship listings and more.

Variety Careers, www.varietycareers.com: This site is a branch of *Variety*, the trade magazine; see below.

Trade Magazines

Variety, www.variety.com

The Hollywood Reporter, www.hollywoodreporter.com

Screen International, www.screendaily.com

These three print and online publications can provide one-stop shopping for research, your quest for employment, and your need to stay current. Premium online services are available for each. Required reading for anyone with any level of aspiration within the entertainment industry.

Appendix E:
The Story Analyst's Checklist

PLOT

✦ Is it full of **conflict**? **Complications**? Major pitfalls?

✦ Does it adhere to its **central conflict**? Is it driven by the hero's main goal?

✦ Does it offer enough **reversals or twists** to keep it interesting and is it well paced?

✦ Is it **predictable**?

✦ Does it **suspend disbelief**? (Does it create rules and stick to them)?

✦ Is there **urgency** to it? What is the **ticking clock**?

✦ Are there any **plot holes**?

STRUCTURE

✦ Does it adhere to the rules of **three-act structure**?

✦ Does **Act I** sufficiently set up who our main character is, what world she's in (the rules), **what's at stake** if she leaves this world/mindset?

✦ Is it clear when the lead character jumps or is pushed into "dangerous new territory" (**first turning point; plot point 1**)?

✦ Does **Act II** offer an engaging series of pitfalls and peaks, while escalating the stakes? (Often the first part of Act II represents a character crawling out of a deep hole or gradually slipping into one.) Is the story refreshed by a thrilling, original and/or revelatory **midpoint** that sends it into a new direction? Does Act II wrap up with a proper reversal, low point, twist, or sub-climax that propels the pace and direction of the rest of the script (**second turning point; plot point 2**)?

✦ Does **Act III** send our hero hurtling toward the "hornets' nest" of his/her innermost fears? Does it present us with a new ticking clock? Does our hero enter a "near-death" situation leading up to a dramatic climax where all is decided, revealed, and ended? Is the resolution short and satisfying, or are you ready to close the script before the writer is done?

✦ OR does the script go out on a limb and experiment with other structural approaches (e.g. **nonlinear; episodic**)? If so, does this approach succeed in maintaining pace while serving character development?

CHARACTER

✦ Is the hero (or heroes) **sympathetic**?

✦ Are the protagonist's **wants and needs** clearly defined?

✦ Does the protagonist complete a **character arc**?

✦ What is at **stake** for the protagonist if she doesn't accomplish her goals? (Are these stakes elevated throughout the story?)

✦ Are the characters **well-rounded**, each with a set of hopes, dreams, fears, quirks, likes, and dislikes? *Is the protagonist humanized by flaw(s) as much as the antagonist is humanized by virtue(s)?*

✦ Do the characters experience a wide range of emotions?

✦ Is the lead character active (i.e., does she make things happen in the plot)?

✦ Is the script character-driven or plot-driven?

SUBPLOT

+ Is the plot enhanced by engaging **subplots** that are spawned by, intersect with, or are resolved by the main storyline?

+ Do these subplots effectively help the plot to breathe with emotion, theme, and character exploration?

+ Do the subplots run through their own progression of beginning-middle-end?

DIALOGUE

+ Is it true-to-life?

+ Does it serve **character distinction**?

+ *Does the author keep in mind that he is writing for a visual medium?*

OTHER

+ **Payoff**: Is it tight? Does everything pay off that has been introduced and vice versa?

+ **Tone**: Is it consistent throughout or does it shift?

+ **Point of View**: Is it consistent throughout or does it shift? If it does change, does it serve a purpose or is it a result of indecisive writing?

+ **Formatting**: Is the material presented in standard format, including: proper scene headings; black, 12-point, Courier font; approximate 1-inch margins in any direction; and centered character names and dialogue?

+ **Style**: Does the narration guide the reader's imagination and not the director's camera?

CONCEPT, MARKETABILITY, AND COMMERCIAL POTENTIAL

✦ Is the concept unique? If not, what other films have followed this course? If so, how will it stand out from anything else that's been done?

✦ Is it **high concept**?

✦ Which classic formula (if any) does it evoke? (Boy Meets Girl; David vs. Goliath; Man vs. Nature; Stranger in a Strange Land; Opposites Attract; Opposites Thrown Together; The Quest; The Secret; Sudden Powers; Coming of Age.)

✦ Would it transport us to another time, place, reality, culture, subculture, and/or perspective?

✦ Is it marketable? Can you imagine an appealing trailer for this film? Can it be compared to other successful films without calling it the same thing?

✦ Who is the **target audience**? If it's not for the **mainstream**, then whom? (Teens? 18- to 29-year-olds? Family/children? Thirty and above? Baby Boomers? Art house? A certain race or ethnicity? Consider male vs. female.) Will it appeal to this group? Is there **crossover potential**?

✦ Considering the **budget** you imagine, would it make sense to make this? (Keep in mind burgeoning home entertainment and international markets.)

✦ Does it offer castable roles?

Appendix F:
Development Notes Guidelines

While templates for notes can vary, these are the guidelines I follow and give to all readers who prepare notes for me. Before you begin development notes for a client or employer, confirm a preferred template. And before that, make sure you have mastered standard coverage.

Your report should total 5–10 pages. Always include a standard top sheet.

AFTER THE TOP SHEET (and synopsis, only if requested) START IN MEMO FORM WITH:

Dear Client:

Here you should offer an overview of the comments to come and, perhaps, point out what in the script *does* work (2–3 short paragraphs).

Then, in your notes you may include general headings about:

PREMISE
CHARACTER
PLOT
STRUCTURE

TONE
POINT OF VIEW
THEME
SETTING
DIALOGUE
PACE
COMMERCIAL POTENTIAL
BELIEVABILITY

. . . and any other story elements you can think of. You are *not* required to include all of them—only those areas in which the script needs work!

Naturally, some of the above elements go hand in hand. Use your judgment as to which category the problem most notably falls under. If the script is very good, you might also offer some positive feedback within the category.

Then, include subheadings followed by specific ideas/instructions (1–4 paragraphs each).

For example, under a **CHARACTERS** heading, you might say:

CLARIFY ROBIN'S ARC
Then go on to specify what's wrong with Robin's arc, why it doesn't work, and how you would recommend fixing it (2–3 paragraphs).

FLESH OUT JOEY'S BACKSTORY
Then go on to specify what's unclear about Joey, why it's important that we have more information, and perhaps some ideas for improvement.

Or under a **STRUCTURE** heading, you might say:

SOLIDIFY THE BEGINNING OF THE THIRD ACT
Point out that it's unclear when Act III begins, the consequent effect this has on the script's pacing, and what you would suggest for changes.

At the end of your notes, include a section for **PAGE NOTES**, which give specific page numbers and comments that don't necessarily fall under any of the above categories but may support what you've stated earlier. Each of these should only be about 1–3 sentences.

Finally, you might also include an **IN CONCLUSION** section to wrap things up (optional).

Appendix G: Filmography

24

A

About Schmidt
Adaptation
Alexander
Alien
Alien vs. Predator
American Pie
Angels in America
Anonymous Rex
Apartment, The
Apocalypse Now
Apostle, The
Artie Lange's Beer League
Assassins
Audrey's Rain
Aviator, The

B

Bad Boys
Battlefield Earth
Bend It Like Beckham
Big Chill, The
Big Fish
Bill
Bill and Ted's Excellent Adventure
Bonnie and Clyde
Boogie Nights

Borat: Cultural Learnings of America for Make Benefit Glorious Nation of Kazakhstan
Bridges of Madison County, The
Brokeback Mountain
Bruce Almighty

C

Chicago
Chronicles of Narnia: The Lion, the Witch and the Wardrobe, The
Cinema Paradiso
Citizen Kane
Click
Crash
Crouching Tiger, Hidden Dragon
Crying Game, The

D

Dangerous Minds
Daughter's Conviction, A
Day After Tomorrow, The
Devil Wears Prada, The
Die Hard
Donnie Brasco
Double Jeopardy
Dragon: The Bruce Lee Story

E

English Patient, The
Erin Brockovich
Eternal Sunshine of the
    Spotless Mind
Eve's Bayou

F

Family Stone, The
Fatal Contact: Bird Flu in
    America
Finding Nemo
First Blood
Forces of Nature
Friday
Fried Green Tomatoes
Fugitive, The
Full Monty, The

G

Garden State
Ghandi
Ghost Dog
Gigli
Girl in the Café, The
Gods and Monsters
Good, The Bad and the Ugly,
    The
Goodfellas
Gosford Park
Graduate, The
Grumpy Old Men

H

Harold & Maude
Harry Potter franchise

Hellboy
Henry Fool
Hours, The
House of the Dead
Hunchback, The
Hustle & Flow

I

Ice Age
Ice Storm, The
Incredibles, The
Inside Man
Iron Jawed Angels
Island, The
Italian Job, The

J

Jaws
Jerry Maguire
John Tucker Must Die
Jumanji

K

Kill Bill
King Kong
Kingdom of Heaven

L

Lady in the Lake
Land Before Time, The
Last Samurai, The
Last Seduction, The
League of Extraordinary
    Gentlemen, The
Legally Blond
Life Is Beautiful

Like Water for Chocolate
Limey, The
Little Miss Sunshine
Lolita
Lord of the Rings trilogy, The
Lorenzo's Oil
Lost in Translation
Love Actually
Love at First Bite
Luzhin Defense, The

M

Magnolia
Man on Fire
Martha Behind Bars
Marvin's Room
Matrix, The
Memoirs of a Geisha
Midnight Cowboy
Midnight Run
Miss Evers' Boys
Mission: Impossible III
Mosquito Coast, The
My Big Fat Greek Wedding
My Family
Mystic River

N

Napoleon Dynamite

P

Passion of the Christ, The
Perfect Storm, The
Pirates of Silicon Valley, The
Pirates of the Caribbean trilogy
Pontiac Moon

Predator
Priest
Psycho
Pulp Fiction

R

Raiders of the Lost Ark
Rain Man
Ray
Requiem for a Dream
Resident Evil
Run Lola Run

S

Saw
Scary Movie
School of Rock
Selena
Shaun of the Dead
Short Cuts
Sideways
Sixth Sense, The
Sleepless in Seattle
Sling Blade
Snow Walker, The
So I Married an Axe Murderer
Solaris
Something's Gotta Give
Sopranos, The
Soul Food
Species III
Spiderman
Squid and the Whale, The
Stand By Me
Star Wars

Author's Biography

From Hollywood to Harvard, Asher Garfinkel has presented his screenplay analysis workshop entitled "The Art and Business of Story Analysis." Over the past fifteen years, Asher has worked in production and development for studios such as New Line Cinema and Paramount, for independent film companies such as Alliance Atlantis and Sun Moon & Stars Entertainment, for feature directors including Peter Medak and Brett Ratner, and for producers like Paul Webster. As a story analyst, he has evaluated thousands of scripts for a multitude of producers, directors, actors, agents, managers, and writers. He is the founder of Readers Unlimited (*www. reader-sunlimited.com*), a Los Angeles-based screenplay coverage and consulting service. Asher holds an MFA in screenwriting from the UCLA School of Theater, Film, and Television.

Index

Books from Allworth Press

Allworth Press is an imprint of Allworth Communications, Inc. Selected titles are listed below.

The Perfect Screenplay: Writing It and Selling It
by Katherine Atwell Herbert (paperback, 6 × 9, 224 pages, $16.95)

The Screenwriter's Legal Guide, Third Edition
by Stephen F. Breimer (paperback, 6 × 9, 352 pages, $24.95)

The Screenwriter's Guide to Agents and Managers
by John Scott Lewinski (paperback, 6 × 9, 256 pages, $18.95)

Writing Television Comedy
by Jerry Rannow (paperback, 6 × 9, 224 pages, $14.95)

Hollywood Dealmaking: Negotiating Talent Agreements
by Dina Appleton and Daniel Yankelevits (paperback, 6 × 9, 256 pages, $19.95)

Producing for Hollywood, Second Edition
by Paul Mason and Don Gold (paperback, 6 × 9, 288 pages, $19.95)

Jumpstart Your Awesome Film Production Company
by Sara Caldwell (paperback, 6 × 9, 208 pages, $19.95)

They'll Never Put That on the Air: The New Age of TV Comedy
by Allan Neuwirth (paperback, 6 × 9, 256 pages, $19.95)

The Health and Safety Guide for Film, TV, and Theatre
by Monona Rossol (paperback, 6 × 9, 256 pages, $19.95)

Get the Picture? The Movie Lover's Guide to Watching Films
by Jim Piper (paperback, 6 × 9, 240 pages, $18.95)

Please write to request our free catalog. To order by credit card, call 1-800-491-2808 or send a check or money order to Allworth Press, 10 East 23rd Street, Suite 510, New York, NY 10010. Include $6 for shipping and handling for the first book ordered and $1 for each additional book. Ten dollars plus $1 for each additional book if ordering from Canada. New York State residents must add sales tax.

To see our complete catalog on the World Wide Web, or to order online, you can find us at ***www.allworth.com.***